COMPUTER SCIENCE, TECHNOLOGY AND APPLICATIONS

AN INSIGHT TO COMPUTERS

COMPUTER SCIENCE, TECHNOLOGY AND APPLICATIONS

Additional books and e-books in this series can be found on Nova's website under the Series tab.

COMPUTER SCIENCE, TECHNOLOGY AND APPLICATIONS

AN INSIGHT TO COMPUTERS

S. ANANDAMURUGAN

Copyright © 2019 by Nova Science Publishers, Inc.

All rights reserved. No part of this book may be reproduced, stored in a retrieval system or transmitted in any form or by any means: electronic, electrostatic, magnetic, tape, mechanical photocopying, recording or otherwise without the written permission of the Publisher.

We have partnered with Copyright Clearance Center to make it easy for you to obtain permissions to reuse content from this publication. Simply navigate to this publication's page on Nova's website and locate the "Get Permission" button below the title description. This button is linked directly to the title's permission page on copyright.com. Alternatively, you can visit copyright.com and search by title, ISBN, or ISSN.

For further questions about using the service on copyright.com, please contact:
Copyright Clearance Center
Phone: +1-(978) 750-8400　　　Fax: +1-(978) 750-4470　　　E-mail: info@copyright.com.

NOTICE TO THE READER

The Publisher has taken reasonable care in the preparation of this book, but makes no expressed or implied warranty of any kind and assumes no responsibility for any errors or omissions. No liability is assumed for incidental or consequential damages in connection with or arising out of information contained in this book. The Publisher shall not be liable for any special, consequential, or exemplary damages resulting, in whole or in part, from the readers' use of, or reliance upon, this material. Any parts of this book based on government reports are so indicated and copyright is claimed for those parts to the extent applicable to compilations of such works.

Independent verification should be sought for any data, advice or recommendations contained in this book. In addition, no responsibility is assumed by the Publisher for any injury and/or damage to persons or property arising from any methods, products, instructions, ideas or otherwise contained in this publication.

This publication is designed to provide accurate and authoritative information with regard to the subject matter covered herein. It is sold with the clear understanding that the Publisher is not engaged in rendering legal or any other professional services. If legal or any other expert assistance is required, the services of a competent person should be sought. FROM A DECLARATION OF PARTICIPANTS JOINTLY ADOPTED BY A COMMITTEE OF THE AMERICAN BAR ASSOCIATION AND A COMMITTEE OF PUBLISHERS.

Additional color graphics may be available in the e-book version of this book.

Library of Congress Cataloging-in-Publication Data

Names: Anandamurugan, S., author.
Title: An insight to computers / S. Anandamurugan, Ph.D., Kongu Engineering
　College, Perundurai, Tamilnadu, India.
Description: Hauppauge, New York: Nova Science Publishers, Inc., [2019] |
　Series: Computer science, technology and applications
Identifiers: LCCN 2019003357 (print) | LCCN 2019004890 (ebook) | ISBN 9781536149869 (ebook) |
ISBN 9781536149852 (softcover)
Subjects: LCSH: Computer science--Popular works.
Classification: LCC QA76 (ebook) | LCC QA76 .A6155 2019 (print) | DDC 004--dc23
LC record available at https://lccn.loc.gov/2019003357

Published by Nova Science Publishers, Inc. † New York

Contents

Preface		**vii**
Chapter 1	Introduction to Computers	**1**
Chapter 2	Components of Computer System	**11**
Chapter 3	Tips and Tricks for Computer	**55**
Chapter 4	How to Assemble a Desktop PC	**129**
Glossary		**149**
Common Filetypes		**153**
Keyboard Shortcuts		**155**
About the Author		**157**
Index		**161**

PREFACE

An Insight to Computers gives an overview of the computers after providing the reader with its brief history. It covers computer applications, advantages, disadvantages, hardware components and software components.

Features:

- Student friendly:written in a clear, concise and lucid manner
- A sincere attempt has been made to introduce the basic concepts
- Each chapter is organized into small sections that address key topics
- In-depth coverage and good style are emphasized
- Motivates the unmotivated
- Covers both elementary as well as advanced concepts
- Aids understanding of concepts by providing diagrams and program listings wherever appropriate
- Logical flow of concepts starting from the preliminary topics to the major topics

This book is intended for use by new students taking courses related to computers. The book is structured as an introductory book, but it is designed to be accessible to a wide audience. This book uses a simple approach for better understanding via the help of diagrams. This book can be used as an introductory text to computers by advanced undergraduate or graduate students in computer science or related disciplines such as computer engineering, computer technology and information technology.

Chapter 1

INTRODUCTION TO COMPUTERS

ABSTRACT

This chapter gives an overview of computers after providing the reader with its brief history. Included are the following:

- Computer definition
- Evolution of computers
- Characteristics of computers
- Classification of computers
- Advantages of computers
- Limitation of computers
- Application of computers

1.1. COMPUTER

- Fast and accurate electronic data manipulating system
- Automatically accept and store input data
- Process and produce output results

- It is done under the direction of a detailed step-by-step stored program of instructions.

1.2. EVOLUTION OF COMPUTERS

1822 *Difference Engine:* Charles Babbage invented a steam-driven calculating machine called Difference Engine to calculate polynomials functions which are used in mathematics and engineering.

1833 *Analytical Engine:* A general-purpose programmable computing machine invented by Charles Babbage which has some essential principles found in the modern digital computers.

1890 *Punch Card System:* Herman Hollerith designed Punch card system to calculate census.

1944 *Harvard Mark:* Howard Aiken designed a series of four calculating machines of increasing sophistication, based on different technologies, from the largely mechanical Mark I to the electronic Mark IV.

1946 *ENIAC (Electronic Numerical Integrator And Computer):* built by John Mauchly was the first large-scale computer to run at electronic speed without being slowed by any mechanical parts.

1948 *EDVAC (Electronic Discrete Variable Automatic Computer):* also built by built by John Mauchly was one of the earliest electronic computers. It was based on the stored program concept proposed by John Von Neumann.

1949 *EDSAC (Electronic Delay Storage Automatic Calculator):* Maurice Wilkes built the EDSAC. It also used the stored-program concept.

1951 *UNIVAC (Universal Automatic Computer):* Mauchly and Presper built the UNIVAC which was the first commercial computer for business and government applications

1953 *IBM 701:* released by IBM. It was the first commercial and mass:produced computer

1960 *PDP-1:* released by Digital Equipment Corporation (DEC) and was a precursor to minicomputer.

1966 *HP 2115:* released by Hewlett Packard and was its first general purpose computer

1975 *Altair 8800:* invented by Ed Roberts which was the first personal computer

1976 *Apple I:* invented by Steve Jobs and Steve Wozniak

1982 *Grid Compass 1101:* designed by Bill Moggridge was the first Laptop computer

2006 *Mac Book Pro:* introduced by Apple and it was a Laptop resulted in more speed than its previous Laptop called PowerBook G4

2010 *Pad:* introduced by Apple which was the first tablet computer.

1.3. CHARACTERISTICS OF COMPUTERS

The following are the characteristics of a modern digital computer:

1.3.1. Speed

A computer has the ability to process data at a faster rate. It can solve a very large and complex problem in a few seconds. The execution speed of a computer is measured in terms of Millions of Instructions Per Second (MIPS).

1.3.2. Accuracy

A computer has the ability to do the calculations accurately. But, the computers produce results according to the instructions given. If a faulty instruction is given to the computer, then faulty results occur. This is known as Garbage In, Garbage Out (GIGO).

1.3.3. Diligence

It is the ability to execute each and every instruction without any tiredness and lack of concentration. Same accuracy and speed is retained throughout the program.

1.3.4. Reliability

A computer has the ability to perform well without any error or failure. A computer generates an error due to wrong instructions given to it by the user.

1.3.5. Storage Capability

It is the ability to store large amounts of data and recall as and when required.

1.3.6. Versatility

It is the ability to perform multiple tasks simultaneously. It is possible to print a document while editing another document.

1.3.7. Resource Sharing

A computer has the ability to share data, information and devices among other computers.

1.4. CLASSIFICATION OF COMPUTERS

Computers can be classified according to the following categories:

1. According to the technology used
   a) First generation computers
   b) Second generation computers
   c) Third generation computers
   d) Fourth generation computers
   e) Fifth generation computers

2. According to the working principles involved
   a) Analog computers
   b) Digital Computers
   c) Hybrid Computers

3. According to the processing capability
   a) Micro computers
   b) Mini computers
   c) Main-frame computers
   d) Super computers

4. According to the field of applications
   a) General purpose computers
   b) Special purpose computers

1.5. ADVANTAGES OF COMPUTERS

- Stores large amounts of data and information
- Ability to perform complex and repetitive calculations rapidly and accurately
- To provide information to user
- To draw and print graphs
- To interact with users through terminals
- Reliability
- It is not time dependent as humans (tireless)
- Processing speed is very high

1.6. LIMITATION OF COMPUTERS

- Lack of common sense
  - The computer is only a tool. It cannot think. It doesn't have common sense or intelligence

- Inability to Correct
  - A computer cannot correct a wrong instruction

- Dependence on human instructions
  - A computer can do what it is told to do. It cannot generate any information on its own

1.7. APPLICATIONS OF COMPUTERS

Computers have their applications everywhere. They find their applications in almost every sphere of life. Computers made our life easier since they provide easy access to the information and faster communication. With the advent of computers, a person can get latest news, ask for a piece of advice, people can shop, book journey tickets, carry out bank transactions etc., without leaving their house.

It also makes our life happier by enabling us to keep in touch with our loved once by means of internet chats, video calls like skype, social networking sites and various applications. It is very difficult to find a field where a computer is of no use. A few of the fields is listed below:

1.7.1. Science

Computers are used for carrying out research and development activities. They are mainly used to develop theories, analyse and test data. They play main role in satellite launching applications. They are also useful in meteorological department for prediction of natural disasters like cyclone etc.

1.7.2. Education

Computers have revolutionized teaching and learning in a big way. Students can have a better learning experience through multimedia tutorials, online libraries, e-books etc. Computer aided Education and Computer based training makes learning more interactive.

1.7.3. Medicine and Health Care

Computers become an essential in every hospital. Everything is computerized today, from open heart surgeries to X-rays to various clinical tests. Computers play a vital role in diagnosing and monitoring the patient's health. Automated imaging technique helps doctor to study human body and functioning of internal organs.

1.7.4. Engineering

Computers can be used in every aspect of the engineering process, from design to production and distribution. Computers are used to create complex designs and drawing which is very difficult to do manually. Computers are also used to project 3D view of the objects. Computer Aided Manufacturing (CAM) is used for designing and planning products.

1.7.5. Entertainment

Computers are very useful in entertainment like playing music, games and videos. They are used to control image and sounds and to produce special effects. They have revolutionized and modernized the way the films are produced. Computers offer wide variety of game, which is the most favorable entertainment for anyone.

1.7.6. Communication

One of the most remarkable achievements of computers is the way the communications are being carried out today. Communication has been modernized with the advent of computers. Data transfer is made so quick with the use of computers in communication. They play a major role in email, blogs, social networking, video chat and Voice-Over-Internet Protocol.

1.7.7. Business Applications

Almost every business uses computers to perform their day-to-day activities. From making contact with clients to inputting data for reports, computers allow business people to manage their activities in a more efficient way. The use of e-mail and Internet has changed the ways in which a business operates. They enable the buyers and sellers contact and carry out the business without any intermediately.

1.7.8. Publishing

Desktop publishing (DTP) combines the use of a personal computer and page layout software to create publication-ready documents. DTP helps us to design and print posters, brochures, books, magazines, news articles, invitations etc. Due to increasing costs and declining interest in traditional paper-based publications, the computers help in offering online editions of many newspapers and magazines.

1.7.9. Banking

Computerized banking is the process by which banking transactions by bank employees and customers are performed electronically, eliminating the need for paper files and physically entering the bank itself. ATM is a facility provided by banks to perform transactions round the clock. Nowadays, banking through internet and mobile is the most useful service provided with the help of computers.

CONCLUSION

This chapter has presented the history, advantages, disadvantages, classification and application of computers.

Chapter 2

COMPONENTS OF COMPUTER SYSTEM

ABSTRACT

This chapter gives an overview of the computer components after providing the reader with its brief introduction. Discussed will be the following

- Computer Units
- Input Unit
- Output Unit
- Central Processing Unit (CPU)
- Memory
- Port
- Software
- Operating System
- Compiler
- Computer Organization

2.1. INTRODUCTION

Computer requires various units to perform the prescribed tasks and to co-ordinate the operations. Basically a computer has four units.

1. Input Unit
2. Output Unit
3. Central Processing Unit (CPU)
4. Memory

2.2. INPUT UNIT

- Input devices are electromechanical devices
- People give data and instructions to the computer through input devices
- Computer accepts input in two ways, either manually or directly
- Manual input is given through keyboard and a mouse
- Direct input is fed to a computer through bar code

Following are some of the important input devices which are used in a computer:

- Keyboard
- Mouse
- Joy Stick
- Light pen
- Track Ball
- Scanner
- Graphic Tablet
- Microphone

- Magnetic Ink Card Reader (MICR)
- Optical Character Reader (OCR)
- Bar Code Reader
- Optical Mark Reader (OMR)

2.2.1. Keyboard

Keyboard is the most common and very popular input device which helps to input data to the computer. The layout of the keyboard is like that of traditional typewriter, although there are some additional keys provided for performing additional functions.

Figure 2.1. Keyboard.

Keyboards are of two sizes 84 keys or 101/102 keys, but now keyboards with 104 keys or 108 keys are also available for Windows and Internet.

The keys on the keyboard are shown in Table 2.1.

Table 2.1. Keys on the keyboard

S. No	Keys & Description
1	*Typing Keys* These keys include the letter keys (A-Z) and digit keys (09) which generally give the same layout as that of typewriters.
2	*Numeric Keypad* It is used to enter the numeric data or cursor movement. Generally, it consists of a set of 17 keys that are laid out in the same configuration used by most adding machines and calculators.
3	*Function Keys* The twelve function keys are present on the keyboard which are arranged in a row at the top of the keyboard. Each function key has a unique meaning and is used for some specific purpose.
4	*Control Keys* These keys provide cursor and screen control. It includes four directional arrow keys. Control keys also include Home, End, Insert, Delete, Page Up, Page Down, Control (Ctrl), Alternate (Alt), Escape (Esc).
5	*Special Purpose Keys* Keyboard also contains some special purpose keys such as Enter, Shift, Caps Lock, Num Lock, Space bar, Tab, and Print Screen.

2.2.2. Mouse

The mouse is the most popular pointing device. It is a very famous cursor-control device having a small palm size box with a round ball at its base, which senses the movement of the mouse and sends corresponding signals to the CPU when the mouse buttons are pressed.

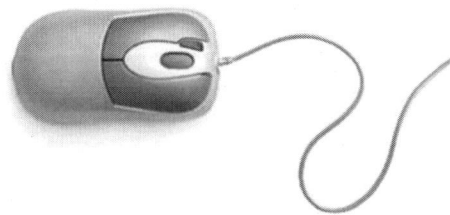

Figure 2.2. Mouse.

Components of Computer System

Generally, it has two buttons called the left and the right button and a wheel is present between the buttons. A mouse can be used to control the position of the cursor on the screen, but it cannot be used to enter text into the computer.

Advantages

- Easy to use
- Not very expensive
- Moves the cursor faster than the arrow keys of the keyboard.

2.2.3. Joystick

The joystick is also a pointing device, which is used to move the cursor position on a monitor screen. It is a stick having a spherical ball at its both lower and upper ends. The lower spherical ball moves in a socket. The joystick can be moved in all four directions.

The function of the joystick is similar to that of a mouse. It is mainly used in Computer Aided Designing (CAD) and playing computer games.

Figure 2.3. Joystick.

2.2.4. Light Pen

Light pen is a pointing device similar to a pen. It is used to select a displayed menu item or draw pictures on the monitor screen. It consists of a photocell and an optical system placed in a small tube.

When the tip of a light pen is moved over the monitor screen and the pen button is pressed, its photocell sensing element detects the screen location and sends the corresponding signal to the CPU.

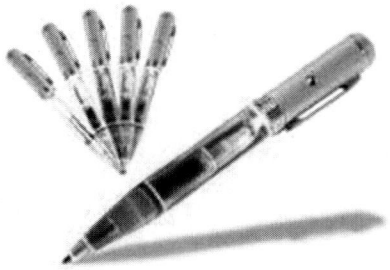

Figure 2.4. Light Pen.

2.2.5. Track Ball

Track ball is an input device that is mostly used in notebook or laptop computer, instead of a mouse. This is a ball which is half inserted and by moving fingers on the ball, the pointer can be moved.

Figure 2.5. Track ball.

Since the whole device is not moved, a track ball requires less space than a mouse. A track ball comes in various shapes like a ball, a button, or a square.

2.2.6. Scanner

Scanner is an input device, which works more like a photocopy machine. It is used when some information is available on paper and it is to be transferred to the hard disk of the computer for further manipulation.

Scanner captures images from the source which are then converted into a digital form that can be stored on the disk. These images can be edited before they are printed.

Figure 2.6. Scanner.

2.2.7. Digitizer

Digitizer is an input device which converts analog information into digital form. Digitizer can convert a signal from the television or camera into a series of numbers that could be stored in a computer. They can be used by the computer to create a picture of whatever the camera had been pointed at.

Figure 2.7. Digitizer.

Digitizer is also known as Tablet or Graphics Tablet as it converts graphics and pictorial data into binary inputs. A graphic tablet as digitizer is used for fine works of drawing and image manipulation applications.

2.2.8. Microphone

Microphone is an input device to input sound that is then stored in a digital form.

The microphone is used for various applications such as adding sound to a multimedia presentation or for mixing music.

Figure 2.8. Microphone.

2.2.9. Magnetic Ink Card Reader (MICR)

MICR input device is generally used in banks as there are large number of cheques to be processed every day. The bank's code number and cheque number are printed on the cheques with a special type of ink that contains particles of magnetic material that are machine readable.

This reading process is called Magnetic Ink Character Recognition (MICR). The main advantages of MICR is that it is fast and less error prone.

Figure 2.9. Magnetic Ink Card Reader (MICR).

2.2.10. Optical Character Reader (OCR)

OCR is an input device used to read a printed text.

OCR scans the text optically, character by character, converts them into a machine readable code, and stores the text on the system memory.

Figure. 2.10. Optical Character Reader (OCR).

2.2.11. Bar Code Readers

Bar Code Reader is a device used for reading bar coded data (data in the form of light and dark lines). Bar coded data is generally used in labelling goods, numbering the books, etc. It may be a handheld scanner or may be embedded in a stationary scanner.

Bar Code Reader scans a bar code image, converts it into an alphanumeric value, which is then fed to the computer that the bar code reader is connected to.

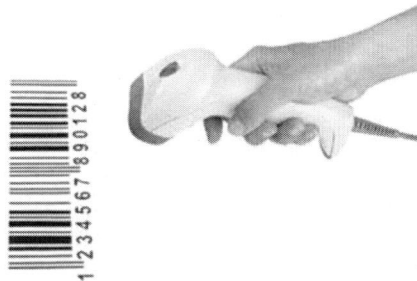

Figure 2.11. Bar Code Readers.

2.2.12. Optical Mark Reader (OMR)

OMR is a special type of optical scanner used to recognize the type of mark made by pen or pencil. It is used where one out of a few alternatives is to be selected and marked.

Figure 2.12. Optical Mark Reader (OMR).

It is specially used for checking the answer sheets of examinations having multiple choice questions.

2.3. OUTPUT DEVICES

- Computers communicate with human beings using output devices
- Output unit displays the processed result to the human
- Output may take one of the two forms:
  - Physical form of output known as hard copy through printers
  - Electronic form of output resides in computer memory known as soft copy

Following are some of the important output devices used in a computer:

- Monitors
- Graphic Plotter
- Printer

2.3.1. Monitors

Monitors, commonly called as Visual Display Unit (VDU), are the main output device of a computer. It forms images from tiny dots, called pixels that are arranged in a rectangular form. The sharpness of the image depends upon the number of pixels.

There are two kinds of viewing screen used for monitors.

- Cathode-Ray Tube (CRT)
- Flat-Panel Display

2.3.1.1. Cathode-Ray Tube (CRT) Monitor

The CRT display is made up of small picture elements called pixels. The smaller the pixels, the better the image clarity or resolution. It takes more than one illuminated pixel to form a whole character, such as the letter 'e' in the word help.

A finite number of characters can be displayed on a screen at once. The screen can be divided into a series of character boxes - fixed location on the screen where a standard character can be placed. Most screens are capable of displaying 80 characters of data horizontally and 25 lines vertically.

There are some disadvantages of CRT:

- Large in Size
- High power consumption

Figure 2.13. Cathode-Ray Tube (CRT) Monitor.

2.3.1.2. Flat-Panel Display Monitor

The flat-panel display refers to a class of video devices that have reduced volume, weight and power requirement in comparison to the

CRT. You can hang them on walls or wear them on your wrists. Current uses of flat-panel displays include calculators, video games, monitors, laptop computer, and graphics display.

Figure 2.14. Flat-Panel Display Monitor.

The flat-panel display is divided into two categories:

- *Emissive Displays* − Emissive displays are devices that convert electrical energy into light. For example, plasma panel and LED (Light-Emitting Diodes).
- *Non-Emissive Displays* − Non-emissive displays use optical effects to convert sunlight or light from some other source into graphics patterns. For example, LCD (Liquid-Crystal Device).

2.3.2. Printers

Printer is an output device, which is used to print information on paper.

There are two types of printers:

- Impact Printers
- Non-Impact Printers

2.3.2.1. Impact Printers

Impact printers print the characters by striking them on the ribbon, which is then pressed on the paper.

Characteristics of Impact Printers are the following:

- Very low consumable costs
- Very noisy
- Useful for bulk printing due to low cost
- There is physical contact with the paper to produce an image

These printers are of two types:

- Character printers
- Line printers

2.3.2.1.1. Character Printers

Character printers are the printers which print one character at a time.

These are further divided into two types:

- Dot Matrix Printer (DMP)
- Daisy Wheel

2.3.2.1.2. Dot Matrix Printer

In the market, one of the most popular printers is Dot Matrix Printer. These printers are popular because of their ease of printing and economical price. Each character printed is in the form of pattern of dots and head consists of a Matrix of Pins of size (5*7, 7*9, 9*7 or 9*9) which come out to form a character which is why it is called Dot Matrix Printer.

Figure 2.15. Dot matrix printer.

Advantages

- Inexpensive
- Widely Used
- Other language characters can be printed

Disadvantages

- Slow Speed
- Poor Quality

2.3.2.1.3. Daisy Wheel

Head is lying on a wheel and pins corresponding to characters are like petals of Daisy (flower) which is why it is called Daisy Wheel Printer. These printers are generally used for word-processing in offices that require a few letters to be sent here and there with very nice quality.

Advantages

- More reliable than DMP
- Better quality
- Fonts of character can be easily changed

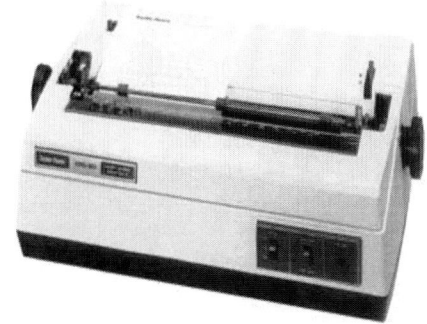

Figure 2.16. Daisy Wheel.

Disadvantages

- Slower than DMP
- Noisy
- More expensive than DMP

2.3.2.1.4. Line Printers

Line printers are the printers which print one line at a time.

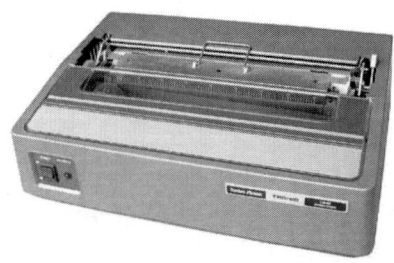

Figure 2.17. Line Printers.

These are of two types:

- Drum Printer
- Chain Printer

2.3.2.1.5. Drum Printer

This printer is like a drum in shape hence it is called drum printer. The surface of the drum is divided into a number of tracks. Total tracks are equal to the size of the paper, i.e., for a paper width of 132 characters, drum will have 132 tracks. A character set is embossed on the track. Different character sets available in the market are 48 character set, 64 and 96 characters set. One rotation of drum prints one line. Drum printers are fast in speed and can print 300 to 2000 lines per minute.

Advantages

- Very high speed

Disadvantages

- Very expensive
- Characters fonts cannot be changed

2.3.2.1.6. Chain Printer

In this printer, a chain of character sets is used, hence it is called Chain Printer. A standard character set may have 48, 64, or 96 characters.

Advantages

- Character fonts can easily be changed.

- Different languages can be used with the same printer.

Disadvantages

- Noisy

2.3.2.2. Non-Impact Printers

Non-impact printers print the characters without using the ribbon. These printers print a complete page at a time, thus they are also called as Page Printers.

These printers are of two types:

- Laser Printers
- Inkjet Printers

2.3.2.2.1. Characteristics of Non-Impact Printers
- Faster than impact printers
- They are not noisy
- High quality
- Supports many fonts and different character size

2.3.2.2.2. Laser Printers

These are non-impact page printers. They use laser lights to produce the dots needed to form the characters to be printed on a page.

Advantages

- Very high speed
- Very high quality output
- Good graphics quality
- Supports many fonts and different character size

Disadvantages

- Expensive
- Cannot be used to produce multiple copies of a document in a single printing

Figure 2.18. Line Printers.

2.3.2.2.3. Inkjet Printers

Inkjet printers are non-impact character printers based on a relatively new technology. They print characters by spraying small drops of ink onto paper. Inkjet printers produce high quality output with presentable features.

Figure 2.19. Inkjet Printers.

They make less noise because no hammering is done and these have many styles of printing modes available. Color printing is also possible. Some models of Inkjet printers can produce multiple copies of printing also.

Advantages

- High quality printing
- More reliable

Disadvantages

- Expensive as the cost per page is high
- Slow as compared to laser printer

2.4. CENTRAL PROCESSING UNIT (CPU)

- It is the brain of a computer system
- CPU processes the input (data) and produces the meaningful information (output)
- CPU consists of three main sub systems:
  a) Arithmetic and Logic Unit
  b) Control Unit
  c) Registers

2.4.1. Arithmetic Logic Unit (ALU)

ALU gets input from registers and performs all arithmetic and logical calculations. It comprises two units:

Components of Computer System

- Arithmetic Unit
- Logic Unit

2.4.1.1. Arithmetic Unit

- It performs arithmetic operations such as addition, subtraction, multiplication and division

2.4.1.2. Logic Unit

- It performs logical operations.
- This unit can compare numbers, letters and take action based on the comparison.
- Logical operations can test for three conditions: equal-to (=) condition, less than condition (<), greater than condition (>).

2.4.1.3. Control Unit (CU)
- It fetches instructions from memory, interprets them and ensures correct execution of the program
- It controls the input/output devices and directs the overall function of other units

2.4.1.4. Registers
- Registers are special purpose, high speed temporary memory units
- They hold various types of information such as data, instructions, addresses and the intermediate results of calculations.
- They are CPU's working memory locations.

2.5. MEMORY

A memory is just like a human brain. It is used to store data and instructions. Computer memory is the storage space in the computer, where data is to be processed and instructions required for processing are stored. The memory is divided into large number of small parts called cells. Each location or cell has a unique address, which varies from zero to memory size minus one. For example, if the computer has 64k words, then this memory unit has 64 * 1024 = 65536 memory locations. The address of these locations varies from 0 to 65535.

Memory is primarily of three types:

- Cache Memory
- Primary Memory/Main Memory
- Secondary Memory

2.5.1. Cache Memory

Cache memory is a very high speed semiconductor memory which can speed up the CPU. It acts as a buffer between the CPU and the main memory. It is used to hold those parts of data and program which are most frequently used by the CPU. The parts of data and programs are transferred from the disk to cache memory by the operating system, from where the CPU can access them.

Advantages

The advantages of cache memory are as follows:
- Cache memory is faster than main memory.
- It consumes less access time as compared to main memory.

- It stores the program that can be executed within a short period of time.
- It stores data for temporary use.

Disadvantages

The disadvantages of cache memory are as follows:

- Cache memory has limited capacity.
- It is very expensive.

Figure 2.20. Cache Memory.

2.5.2. Primary Memory (Main Memory)

Primary memory holds only those data and instructions on which the computer is currently working. It has a limited capacity and data is lost when power is switched off. It is generally made up of semiconductor device. These memories are not as fast as registers. The data and instruction required to be processed resides in the main memory. It is divided into two subcategories RAM and ROM.

Figure 2.21. Main Memory.

Characteristics of Main Memory

- These are semiconductor memories.
- It is known as the main memory.
- Usually volatile memory.
- Data is lost in case power is switched off.
- It is the working memory of the computer.
- Faster than secondary memories.
- A computer cannot run without the primary memory.

2.5.3. Secondary Memory

This type of memory is also known as external memory or non-volatile. It is slower than the main memory. These are used for storing data/information permanently. CPU directly does not access these memories, instead they are accessed via input-output routines. The contents of secondary memories are first transferred to the main memory, and then the CPU can access it. For example, disk, CD-ROM, DVD, etc.

Components of Computer System

Figure 2.22. Secondary Memory.

Characteristics of Secondary Memory:

- These are magnetic and optical memories.
- It is known as the backup memory.
- It is a non-volatile memory.
- Data is permanently stored even if power is switched off.
- It is used for storage of data in a computer.
- Computer may run without the secondary memory.
- Slower than primary memories.

RAM (Random Access Memory) is the internal memory of the CPU for storing data, program, and program result. It is a read/write memory which stores data until the machine is working. As soon as the machine is switched off, data is erased.

Access time in RAM is independent of the address, that is, each storage location inside the memory is as easy to reach as other locations and takes the same amount of time. Data in the RAM can be accessed randomly but it is very expensive.

RAM is volatile, i.e., data stored in it is lost when we switch off the computer or if there is a power failure. Hence, a backup Uninterruptible Power System (UPS) is often used with computers. RAM is small, both in terms of its physical size and in the amount of data it can hold.

RAM is of two types:

- Static RAM (SRAM)
- Dynamic RAM (DRAM)

2.5.3.1. *Static RAM (SRAM)*

The word static indicates that the memory retains its contents as long as power is being supplied. However, data is lost when the power gets down due to volatile nature. SRAM chips use a matrix of 6-transistors and no capacitors. Transistors do not require power to prevent leakage, so SRAM need not be refreshed on a regular basis.

There is extra space in the matrix, hence SRAM uses more chips than DRAM for the same amount of storage space, making the manufacturing costs higher. SRAM is thus used as cache memory and has very fast access.

Characteristic of Static RAM:

- Long life
- No need to refresh
- Faster
- Used as cache memory
- Large size
- Expensive
- High power consumption

2.5.3.2. *Dynamic RAM (DRAM)*

DRAM, unlike SRAM, must be continually refreshed in order to maintain the data. This is done by placing the memory on a refresh circuit that rewrites the data several hundred times per second. DRAM is used for most system memory as it is cheap and small. All DRAMs are made up of memory cells, which are composed of one capacitor and one transistor.

Characteristics of Dynamic RAM:

- Short data lifetime
- Needs to be refreshed continuously
- Slower as compared to SRAM
- Used as RAM
- Smaller in size
- Less expensive
- Less power consumption

ROM stands for Read Only Memory. The memory from which we can only read but cannot write on it. This type of memory is non-volatile. The information is stored permanently in such memories during manufacture. A ROM stores such instructions that are required to start a computer. This operation is referred to as bootstrap. ROM chips are not only used in the computer but also in other electronic items like washing machine and microwave oven.

Let us now discuss the various types of ROMs and their characteristics.

2.5.3.3. MROM (Masked ROM)

The very first ROMs were hard-wired devices that contained a pre-programmed set of data or instructions. These kind of ROMs are known as masked ROMs, which are inexpensive.

2.5.3.4. PROM (Programmable Read Only Memory)

PROM is read-only memory that can be modified only once by a user. The user buys a blank PROM and enters the desired contents using a PROM program. Inside the PROM chip, there are small fuses which are burnt open during programming. It can be programmed only once and is not erasable.

2.5.3.5. EPROM (Erasable and Programmable Read Only Memory)

EPROM can be erased by exposing it to ultra-violet light for a duration of up to 40 minutes. Usually, an EPROM eraser achieves this function. During programming, an electrical charge is trapped in an insulated gate region. The charge is retained for more than 10 years because the charge has no leakage path. For erasing this charge, ultra-violet light is passed through a quartz crystal window (lid). This exposure to ultra-violet light dissipates the charge. During normal use, the quartz lid is sealed with a sticker.

2.5.3.6. EEPROM (Electrically Erasable and Programmable Read Only Memory)

EEPROM is programmed and erased electrically. It can be erased and reprogrammed about ten thousand times. Both erasing and programming take about 4 to 10 ms (millisecond). In EEPROM, any location can be selectively erased and programmed. EEPROMs can be erased one byte at a time, rather than erasing the entire chip. Hence, the process of reprogramming is flexible but slow.

Advantages of ROM

The advantages of ROM are as follows:

- Non-volatile in nature
- Cannot be accidentally changed
- Cheaper than RAMs
- Easy to test
- More reliable than RAMs
- Static and do not require refreshing
- Contents are always known and can be verified

Components of Computer System

The motherboard serves as a single platform to connect all of the parts of a computer together. It connects the CPU, memory, hard drives, optical drives, video card, sound card, and other ports and expansion cards directly or via cables. It can be considered as the backbone of a computer.

Features of Motherboard
A motherboard comes with following features:

- Motherboard varies greatly in supporting various types of components.
- Motherboard supports a single type of CPU and few types of memories.
- Video cards, hard disks, sound cards have to be compatible with the motherboard to function properly.
- Motherboards, cases, and power supplies must be compatible to work properly together.

Popular Manufacturers
Following are the popular manufacturers of the motherboard.

- Intel
- ASUS
- AOpen
- ABIT
- Biostar
- Gigabyte
- MSI

2.5.3.7. Description of Motherboard

The motherboard is mounted inside the case and is securely attached via small screws through pre-drilled holes. Motherboard contains ports to connect all of the internal components. It provides a single socket for CPU, whereas for memory, normally one or more slots are available. Motherboards provide ports to attach the floppy drive, hard drive, and optical drives via ribbon cables. Motherboard carries fans and a special port designed for power supply.

There is a peripheral card slot in front of the motherboard using which video cards, sound cards, and other expansion cards can be connected to the motherboard.

On the left side, motherboards carry a number of ports to connect the monitor, printer, mouse, keyboard, speaker, and network cables. Motherboards also provide USB ports, which allow compatible devices to be connected in plug-in/plug-out fashion. For example, pen drive, digital cameras, etc.

Memory unit is the amount of data that can be stored in the storage unit. This storage capacity is expressed in terms of Bytes.

Table 2.2 explains the main memory storage units.

Table 2.2. The main memory storage units

S. No.	Unit & Description
1	Bit (Binary Digit) A binary digit is logical 0 and 1 representing a passive or an active state of a component in an electric circuit.
2	Nibble A group of 4 bits is called nibble.
3	Byte A group of 8 bits is called byte. A byte is the smallest unit, which can represent a data item or a character.
4	Word A computer word, like a byte, is a group of fixed number of bits processed as a unit, which varies from computer to computer but is fixed for each computer. The length of a computer word is called word-size or word length. It may be as small as 8 bits or may be as long as 96 bits. A computer stores the information in the form of computer words.

Components of Computer System 41

Table 2.3 lists some higher storage units.

Table 2.3. Higher storage units

S. No.	Unit & Description
1	Kilobyte (KB) 1 KB = 1024 Bytes
2	Megabyte (MB) 1 MB = 1024 KB
3	GigaByte (GB) 1 GB = 1024 MB
4	TeraByte (TB) 1 TB = 1024 GB
5	PetaByte (PB) 1 PB = 1024 TB

2.6. OTHER COMPONENTS

2.6.1. Port

A port is a physical docking point using which an external device can be connected to the computer. It can also be programmatic docking point through which information flows from a program to the computer or over the Internet.

2.6.1.1. Characteristics of Ports

A port has the following characteristics:

- External devices are connected to a computer using cables and ports.
- Ports are slots on the motherboard into which a cable of external device is plugged in.

- Examples of external devices attached via ports are the mouse, keyboard, monitor, microphone, speakers, etc.

Let us now discuss a few important types of ports:

Serial Port

- Used for external modems and older computer mouse
- Two versions: 9 pin, 25 pin model
- Data travels at 115 kilobits per second

Parallel Port

- Used for scanners and printers
- Also called printer port
- 25 pin model
- IEEE 1284-compliant Centronics port

PS/2 Port

- Used for old computer keyboard and mouse
- Also called mouse port
- Most of the old computers provide two PS/2 port, each for the mouse and keyboard
- IEEE 1284-compliant Centronics port

Universal Serial Bus (or USB) Port

- It can connect all kinds of external USB devices such as external hard disk, printer, scanner, mouse, keyboard, etc.
- It was introduced in 1997.
- Most of the computers provide two USB ports as minimum.

- Data travels at 12 megabits per seconds.
- USB compliant devices can get power from a USB port.

VGA Port

- Connects monitor to a computer's video card.
- It has 15 holes.
- Similar to the serial port connector. However, serial port connector has pins, VGA port has holes.

Power Connector

- Three-pronged plug.
- Connects to the computer's power cable that plugs into a power bar or wall socket.

Firewire Port

- Transfers large amount of data at very fast speed.
- Connects camcorders and video equipment to the computer.
- Data travels at 400 to 800 megabits per seconds.
- Invented by Apple.
- It has three variants: 4-Pin FireWire 400 connector, 6-Pin FireWire 400 connector, and 9-Pin FireWire 800 connector.

Modem Port

- Connects a PC's modem to the telephone network.

Ethernet Port

- Connects to a network and high speed Internet.
- Connects the network cable to a computer.
- This port resides on an Ethernet Card.
- Data travels at 10 megabits to 1000 megabits per seconds depending upon the network bandwidth.

Game Port

- Connect a joystick to a PC
- Now replaced by USB

Digital Video Interface, DVI port

- Connects Flat panel LCD monitor to the computer's high-end video graphic cards.
- Very popular among video card manufacturers.

Sockets

- Sockets connect the microphone and speakers to the sound card of the computer.

2.7. SOFTWARE

It is a set of programs, which is designed to perform a well-defined function. A program is a sequence of instructions written to solve a particular problem.

There are two types of software:

- System Software
- Application Software

2.7.1. System Software

The system software is a collection of programs designed to operate, control, and extend the processing capabilities of the computer itself. System software is generally prepared by the computer manufacturers. These software products comprise of programs written in low-level languages, which interact with the hardware at a very basic level. System software serves as the interface between the hardware and the end users.

Some examples of system software are Operating System, Compilers, Interpreter, Assemblers, etc.

Here is a list of some of the most prominent features of a system software:

- Close to the system
- Fast in speed
- Difficult to design
- Difficult to understand
- Less interactive
- Smaller in size

- Difficult to manipulate
- Generally written in low-level language

2.7.2. Application Software

Application software products are designed to satisfy a particular need of a particular environment. All software applications prepared in the computer lab can come under the category of Application software.

Application software may consist of a single program, such as Microsoft's notepad for writing and editing a simple text. It may also consist of a collection of programs, often called a software package, which work together to accomplish a task, such as a spreadsheet package.

Examples of Application software are the following:

- Payroll Software
- Student Record Software
- Inventory Management Software
- Income Tax Software
- Railways Reservation Software
- Microsoft Office Suite Software
- Microsoft Word
- Microsoft Excel
- Microsoft PowerPoint

Features of application software are as follows:

- Close to the user
- Easy to design
- More interactive
- Slow in speed

- Generally written in high-level language
- Easy to understand
- Easy to manipulate and use
- Bigger in size and requires large storage space

2.8. OPERATING SYSTEM

The Operating System is a program with the following features:

- An operating system is a program that acts as an interface between the software and the computer hardware.
- It is an integrated set of specialized programs used to manage overall resources and operations of the computer.
- It is a specialized software that controls and monitors the execution of all other programs that reside in the computer, including application programs and other system software.

2.8.1. Objectives of Operating System

The objectives of the operating system are:

- To make the computer system convenient to use in an efficient manner.
- To hide the details of the hardware resources from the users.
- To provide users a convenient interface to use the computer system.
- To act as an intermediary between the hardware and its users, making it easier for the users to access and use other resources.
- To manage the resources of a computer system.

- To keep track of who is using which resource, granting resource requests, and mediating conflicting requests from different programs and users.
- To provide efficient and fair sharing of resources among users and programs.

2.8.2. Characteristics of Operating System

Here is a list of some of the most prominent characteristic features of Operating Systems:

- Memory Management − Keeps track of the primary memory, i.e., what part of it is in use by whom, what part is not in use, etc. and allocates the memory when a process or program requests it.
- Processor Management − Allocates the processor (CPU) to a process and deallocates the processor when it is no longer required.
- Device Management − Keeps track of all the devices. This is also called I/O controller that decides which process gets the device, when, and for how much time.
- File Management − Allocates and de-allocates the resources and decides who gets the resources.
- Security − Prevents unauthorized access to programs and data by means of passwords and other similar techniques.
- Job Accounting − Keeps track of time and resources used by various jobs and/or users.
- Control over System Performance − Records delays between the request for a service and from the system.
- Interaction with the Operators − Interaction may take place via the console of the computer in the form of instructions. The

Components of Computer System 49

Operating System acknowledges the same, does the corresponding action, and informs the operation by a display screen.
- Error-detecting Aids − Production of dumps, traces, error messages, and other debugging and error-detecting methods.
- Coordination between Other Software and Users − Coordination and assignment of compilers, interpreters, assemblers, and other software to the various users of the computer systems.

2.9. COMPILER

A compiler that converts machine language into high-level natural language is called a decompiler. Compilers that produce the object code meant to run on a system are called cross-compilers. Finally, a compiler that converts one programming language into another is called a language translator.

A compiler executes four major steps:

- Scanning: The scanner reads one character at a time from the source code and keeps track of which character is present in which line.
- Lexical Analysis: The compiler converts the sequence of characters that appear in the source code into a series of strings of characters (known as tokens), which are associated by a specific rule by a program called a lexical analyzer. A symbol table is used by the lexical analyzer to store the words in the source code that correspond to the token generated.
- Syntactic Analysis: In this step, syntax analysis is performed, which involves preprocessing to determine whether the tokens created during lexical analysis are in proper order as per their

usage. The correct order of a set of keywords, which can yield a desired result, is called syntax. The compiler has to check the source code to ensure syntactic accuracy.

- Semantic Analysis: This step is comprised of several intermediate steps. First, the structure of tokens is checked, along with their order with respect to the grammar in a given language. The meaning of the token structure is interpreted by the parser and analyzer to finally generate an intermediate code, called object code. The object code includes instructions that represent the processor action for a corresponding token when encountered in the program. Finally, the entire code is parsed and interpreted to check if any optimizations are possible. Once optimizations can be performed, the appropriate modified tokens are inserted in the object code to generate the final object code, which is saved inside a file.

2.10. Basic Computer Organization

In general, all computers perform the following activities:

a) Input: It involves putting information into the system.
b) Process: It involves doing something with the information.
c) Output: It involves displaying results.

The input-process-output activities can be explained with real life examples.

For a tea maker, the activities are as follows:

INPUT	PROCESS	OUTPUT
Tea powder, Sugar, Milk	Heat	Tea

Components of Computer System

The above mentioned activitiy can be accomplished with the following parts of a computer.

- Input Unit
- Central Processing Unit (CPU)/Processing Unit
- Output Unit
- Memory/Storage Unit

The basic organization of a computer is shown in Figure 2.20.

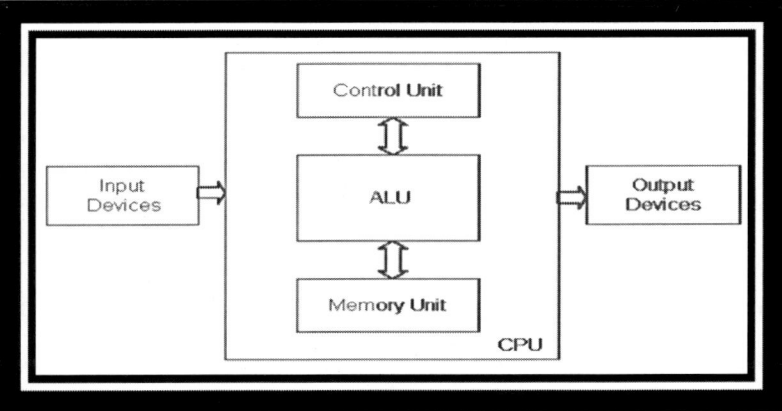

Figure 2.20. Computer Organization.

2.10.1. Input

This is the process of entering data and programs in to the computer system.

2.10.2. Storage

The process of saving data and instructions permanently is known as storage. Data has to be fed into the system before the actual processing starts. It is because the processing speed of Central Processing Unit (CPU) is so fast that the data has to be provided to CPU with the same speed. Therefore the data is first stored in the storage unit for faster access and processing. This storage unit or the primary storage of the computer system is designed to do the above functionality. It provides space for storing data and instructions.

The storage unit performs the following major functions:

- All data and instructions are stored here before and after processing.
- Intermediate results of processing are also stored here.

2.10.3. Processing

The task of performing operations like arithmetic and logical operations is called processing. The Central Processing Unit (CPU) takes data and instructions from the storage unit and makes all sorts of calculations based on the instructions given and the type of data provided. It is then sent back to the storage unit.

2.10.4. Output

This is the process of producing results from the data for getting useful information. Similarly the output produced by the computer after processing must also be kept somewhere inside the computer before being given to you in human readable form. Again the output is also stored inside the computer for further processing.

2.10.5. Control

The manner how instructions are executed and the above operations are performed. Controlling of all operations like input, processing and output are performed by control unit. It takes care of step by step processing of all operations inside the computer.

2.11. FUNCTIONAL UNITS

In order to carry out the operations mentioned in the previous section the computer allocates the task between its various functional units. The computer system is divided into three separate units for its operation. They are 1) arithmetic logical unit, 2) control unit, and 3) central processing unit.

2.11.1. Arithmetic Logical Unit (ALU)

After you enter data through the input device it is stored in the primary storage unit. The actual processing of the data and instruction are performed by Arithmetic Logical Unit. The major operations performed by the ALU are addition, subtraction, multiplication, division, logic and comparison. Data is transferred to ALU from storage unit when required. After processing the output is returned back to storage unit for further processing or getting stored.

2.11.2. Control Unit (CU)

The next component of computer is the Control Unit, which acts like the supervisor seeing that things are done in proper fashion. The control unit determines the sequence in which computer programs and instructions are executed. Things like processing of programs stored in the main memory, interpretation of the instructions and issuing of signals for other units of the computer to execute them. It also acts as a switch board operator when several users access the computer simultaneously. Thereby it coordinates the activities of computer's peripheral equipment as they perform the input and output. Therefore it is the manager of all operations mentioned in the previous section.

2.11.3. Central Processing Unit (CPU)

The ALU and the CU of a computer system are jointly known as the central processing unit. You may call CPU as the brain of any computer system. It is just like brain that takes all major decisions, makes all sorts of calculations and directs different parts of the computer functions by activating and controlling the operations.

CONCLUSION

In this chapter, you have studied the computer components like input unit, output unit, central processing unit, memory and ports. Also you have discussed about computer organization, software, operating system and compiler.

Chapter 3

TIPS AND TRICKS FOR COMPUTER

ABSTRACT

In this chapter we give an overview of how to purchase the computer, purchasing process of computers, insight to computer components, quick tips about computers, common problems encountered in computers and useful web sites for computers. We will discuss:

- Purchase process computer units
- Installation
- Tips on computer maintenance
- Common problems encountered in computers
- Useful links for computers

3.1. HOW TO PURCHASE A COMPUTER

3.1.1. First Steps

Before beginning your search for your new computer:

- Decide if you want a desktop PC or laptop (desktop PCs are more powerful but laptops are portable).
- Decide how much approximately you want to spend.
- Decide what you will be using the PC for (you won't need a particularly powerful system if you're only going to browse the Web and send e-mails).
- Read some computer buying advice magazines such as *What PC?*, *PC Advisor* and *Personal Computer World*.
- Talk to friends, relatives and colleagues about where they bought their PCs from and their experiences.

3.1.2. Where to Buy From

High-street stores may seem the most obvious place for first-time PC buyers but although they do offer some advantages (such as being able to see and touch example PCs and get an idea of the size of the screen) they are not always good value and you may find yourself spending more than you need to.

Often the sales person will also try to sell you warranty packages. These may provide some peace of mind, including things like health checks and repairs, but if you look after your PC and keep your security software up-to-date, you will most likely never use the service and will have paid a lot of extra money for nothing.

You could try small local computer shops that can often put together a PC package to suit your exact needs, though you may find the price a lot higher than the standard packages offered by high-street stores. For first-time buyers a standard package often seems far simpler than trying to figure out the specific types of components you need.

Buying online is often the best option; though obviously you need to find some way of getting on the Internet (on a friend's PC or at your local library) and then begin the process of searching for online stores and comparing packages and prices. As with any large purchase you make, you will want to be cautious and have all the facts in front of you before you make a decision.

3.1.3. What to Look For

Often when reading about PC packages you will be confronted with a huge list of specifications which will mean nothing to you if you don't have much knowledge of computer hardware. Some companies may try to confuse you with technical details, hoping that by mentioning large enough numbers you will think the PC is better than it really is. Computer specifications change all the time and your needs will determine what size or speed components are appropriate for you. The following is a general guide with some tips on what to look for:

- *Monitor* - it is important to check this is mentioned as although this may seem like an essential part of a PC system, some packages may not include one. TFT (Flat Panel) monitors are common nowadays because of how thin they are compared to the old bulky CRT monitors. When buying a monitor you want the highest resolution, which will give a more detailed and sharper picture. A resolution of 1280 x 1024 should be fine for most users. Response time is also important - the lower the number, the better.
- *Keyboard/Mouse* - all desktop PCs should include these and there is often little difference between the various models. One thing to note is that some have more than just the left and right buttons on the Mouse - they often also include a Wheel in the center which can be a useful addition. Nowadays you can also get wireless keyboards and mice. If you want to use a mouse

with your laptop you may need to buy it separately, as many laptops use a touch pad system instead of a mouse.

- *Floppy Disk Drive* - once a standard for all PCs, these are now increasingly rare so decide if you need one. Floppy disks have very small storage space and are not really big enough for most files you will work with. CDs, DVDs and data devices are more suitable for modern data storage and backup purposes.
- *Tower Unit* - the shell of the desktop PC contains all the components which make your system work including the processor, memory and Hard Disk. You should check how many USB ports are included, as you will need one for each peripheral you connect such as scanners and printers.
- *Processor* - the heart of your PC, this is the engine that powers your computer and processes all the instructions it is given, therefore you want it to be as fast as possible. The higher the processor speed (in Ghz) the faster your PC should be. Examples are Intel Pentium or Celeron, and AMD Athlon or Sempron.
- *RAM* - the temporary memory the computer uses to do its calculations. The more RAM you have, the faster and more efficient your programs will run. Look for at least 512 MB of RAM.
- *Hard Disk* - where all your programs and data are stored. As usual, more is better. At least 60GB or more will be needed to store lots of music, games or movie files. You may see packages with huge amounts of hard disk space - this is because it is a fairly cheap way of making a package sound better, when really most users will never need that much disk space.
- *Graphics Card* - handles video and display calculations. A more powerful card means better quality video graphics and smooth-running games. The most popular cards are the NVidia GeForce and ATI Radeon series. Another thing to note is that the

graphics card also has its own RAM memory, and again the more the better.
- *Sound Card* - most PCs should include decent enough sound for playing music or video, but you can opt for better quality sound cards such as the Creative Audigy series which will improve sound quality and performance in movies and demanding games.
- *Speakers* - 2 normal desktop speakers should be fine for most users, but games players may want to invest in larger set-ups such as 5.1 (5 small Satellite speakers and 1 large Sub-Woofer to handle the bass sounds).
- *CD/DVD-ROM Drive* - plays CDs/DVDs including data discs, music CDs and film DVDs. The higher the speed, the faster files will be loaded from disc though it will depend on the maximum speed permitted by the disc itself. '16x,' for example, means it can transfer data from the disc at 16 times the normal playing speed.
- *CD/DVD R/RW Writer/Burner Drive* - as with CD/DVD-ROM Drives but also able to write or 'burn' discs as well as read them. This way you can create your own data, music or video discs, especially useful for backing up large amounts of data. There are two main categories of writeable discs: Recordable discs such as CD-R or DVD-R or DVD+R are discs that can only be written once and Re-Writeable discs such as CD-RW or DVD-RW or DVD+RW can be written over many times like a blank video cassette.
- *Internet Access* - many packages come with free Internet trials, but you can choose a different provider if you find a better deal. To access the Internet from home you will need to connect your PC to your phone line. There should be instructions with your PC how to do this. There are many different Internet packages available, and with some you will need to buy additional

equipment. To learn more, contact an ISP (Internet Service Provider) or visit their web site.
- *Wireless Internet* - PCs and especially laptops may come with built-in wireless support, to allow you to connect to any wireless Internet networks within range. If not, wireless adapters can be bought separately.

3.2. INSIGHT TO COMPUTER COMPONENTS

3.2.1. The Mouse

Most PC users will spend more time using one particular device to interact with their computer than any other, even the Keyboard. The Mouse is primarily used to move the pointer arrow around the screen and to select and activate options.

Beginner computer users often find that using a mouse for the first time is a little tricky - especially when it comes to what to do when the mouse reaches the edge of the mat, but you're on-screen pointer still has further to go.

The idea is that when the mouse is not on the mat, it isn't sending any instructions to the pointer. So to move the pointer all the way across the screen you should slide the mouse along to the edge of the mat, then lift the mouse up off the mat by a few centimeters, place the mouse back down and repeat the same sliding motion again until your pointer reaches the edge of the screen.

Practice moving your pointer in 'circles' around the screen to get a feel for the mouse. Begin with small gentle circular movements and then get faster and wider, drawing a larger circle on the mat and on-screen. You should find that the faster you move the mouse the more distance you cover on-screen.

Tips and Tricks for Computer 61

The mouse buttons are used to interact with whatever is on the screen where the pointer is located. The left mouse button is the one you will use most often. Clicking this tells the PC to select an item and is called 'left-clicking.' To activate an item and use it, you will often need to click the button twice or 'double-click.'

Left-clicking on text in a document will place a flashing cursor at that point, which allows you to begin typing there. If you click and hold the left button and move the mouse, this has the effect of 'dragging' an object about the screen until you release the button.

The right mouse button is often used to bring up a small menu window that gives options specific to the item. To use a particular option you just left-click it. So for example, 'right-clicking' on a song would give you options to play the song in various music programs. Move your pointer to the *Play* option and left-click to start playing.

Common right-click menu options for an item include: *Open* (activate - same as if you double-click), *Cut* (remove to be placed elsewhere), *Copy* (make a copy), *Create Shortcut* (create an icon elsewhere to give quick access), *Delete* (remove permanently), *Rename* (give a new name), and *Properties* (find out information). You may have a third smaller button in the center of your mouse that can be rolled forwards and backwards. This mouse-wheel can be used to move up and down through documents.

3.2.2. The Keyboard

Keyboards can come in a number of different layouts. QWERTY keyboards are so-called because the top line of letters, underneath the number line, begins with those six letters.

There are a number of other useful keys too. The *Enter* key confirms a selection, and pressing the *Shift* and *Caps Lock* keys activates uppercase letters when you type or the special characters above the number keys.

There are several function keys beginning with *F1, F2* and these are used to access different options in different programs. Other keys such as *Home, End* and *Page Up* and *Page Down* allow you to quickly move about within a document.

The arrow keys move the text typing cursor up, down, left or right. You may have a number keypad too. This acts as an alternative to the number keys above the main letter keys. Pressing the *Num Lock* button will switch between using the keypad as numbers keys, or arrow keys.

3.2.3. The Desktop

The Desktop is the main background on your screen when you are working on your PC. It consists of a background picture or 'wallpaper,' any program shortcuts you have created, and the Taskbar.

The Taskbar runs along the bottom of the screen (or the side, or top - you can click and drag it wherever you want to place it) and shows the date and time as well as giving you access to the Start menu. You can also put program shortcuts on the taskbar so that one click will activate a particular program.

Left-clicking on the *Start menu* brings up the *All Programs* list of shortcuts to programs you have on your computer. These are often arranged in 'folders,' so that you can find all the programs made by one company under a folder in their name.

By holding the mouse pointer over a folder you will see a new list appear of whatever programs are within that folder. Some programs will have several related entries - so you might see a README (a document that has instructions for using the program), or an option to *Uninstall* (remove the program from your PC).

You can access your Desktop settings by right-clicking anywhere on the background wallpaper and then clicking on *Properties*.

3.2.4. Windows

The operating system that runs all your programs and allows you to easily interact with your PC is called Windows for a reason. It allows you to work with several different items and programs at once, all in their own 'window.' A window is like a smaller screen contained within a box on your main screen.

When you are working with a window it is brought to the 'front' of the screen, overlapping the Desktop and any other items behind it, so that you can focus on whatever is in the window.

In this way, you can have several windows open at the same time containing different programs that can be opened, closed, and re-arranged across the screen. This means you can do multiple tasks at the same time, such as playing your favourite music while writing an e-mail for example.

3.2.5. Files and Folders

Every item on your PC, whether it is a document, picture, song, game or whatever, is a file that is stored on your computer's Hard Disk. A file can only be activated by programs that understand and are able to use it.

For example, you cannot use a music program to open a letter document. Each program on your computer understands what type of file it can or cannot use by the fact that every file has a filetype given to it.

This takes the form of a few extra letters or numbers added on to its name after a full stop. So for example, 'myletter.doc' is a file named 'myletter' with a filetype. 'doc,' meaning it will require a program that understands doc (document) files, such as Microsoft Word.

Any one single program or application can actually consist of many different files, all working together to achieve the same task. This means modern computers can have millions of files spread across different locations. Folders help organize these files so that for each particular program there can be one folder that contains just the files it needs.

Some folders will contain other folders inside them called 'sub-folders.' For example, to organise your holiday pictures together you might have a folder called 'Holidays 2006' and then other sub-folders within that for each particular holiday destination.

You can take a look at an example of a folder now. On your Desktop you should see a shortcut icon called *My Documents*. Double-clicking this will open a new window showing the contents of the My Documents folder.

3.2.6. My Documents

My Documents is a folder on your computer that is automatically created by Windows, so that you can store all your own files in one place separate from all the other program and system files Windows uses, making them easier to find.

Double-click the *My Documents* shortcut on the Desktop and you will see a list of folders, within which are your files. To see what is inside a folder, double-click on it and the current window will change to show the contents.

Windows and other programs automatically create folders to help you store certain types of files - so you may see folders such as *My*

Music, *My Pictures* and *My Videos*. However, you do not have to use these - you can store any of your files anywhere you want to. You don't even have to use My Documents.

3.2.7. My Computer

Close the current window by clicking the X button in the top-right. On your Desktop, double-click the *My Computer* shortcut and you will see a list of locations where files are stored on your PC.

If you double-click the *Local Disk* (your Hard Disk, usually C:) you can see all the folders of files that are stored on your Hard Disk. The *Program Files* and *Windows* folders here are especially important, and should not be changed as they contain the files necessary for programs and Windows to run.

All files take up disk space and your computer only has so much room to store them all. If you want to see how much of your Hard Disk you have used up so far, and how much space you have left, double-click *My Computer* again and this time, instead of double-clicking the *Local Disk,* right-click and select *Properties.*

If you right-click the My Computer icon on the Desktop rather than double-clicking it, and then click on *Properties,* you can see detailed information about your PC including your hardware devices and performance settings.

3.2.8. The Control Panel

The Control Panel is a collection of all the important options you will need when you want to change settings on your computer. You can find control icons for display, sound, Internet, hardware, programs, security and system settings. To access the Control Panel, click the *Start menu* and then click *Control Panel.*

Changing settings in the Control Panel can make big changes to your PC's setup. For example, the Appearance and Themes or Display options in the Control Panel can affect the quality of your screen and the size of text.

Click on your *Start Menu* and then *Help and Support* for more help with using your PC and particular Windows features.

3.3. QUICK TIPS ABOUT COMPUTERS

3.3.1. Quick Web Address

Type the name of a web site such as 'myspace' into your browser's address bar and press *CTRL+Enter* to automatically add *http://www* and *.com* and be taken to the site.

3.3.2. Save a Web Page Picture

To copy a picture from a web site on to your computer, right-click the image and select *Save Image As* or *Save Picture As.*

3.3.3. Move between Web Links

Use *Tab* and *Shift+Tab* to move between links on a web page and press *Enter* to follow the selected link.

3.3.4. Change the Clock

Double click on the clock on the Taskbar to change the time and date shown. Save web video clips.

To download video clips embedded on a web page, in Firefox right-click the page and select *View Page Info* then click the *Media* tab. Select the video file and click *Save As*.

3.3.5. Check Hard Disk Space

Double click on the *My Computer* icon on your desktop and right-click on your hard disk (usually drive C). Click *Properties* to see the amount of disk space left on your computer.

3.3.6. Create a Web Shortcut

Right-click on a web page in your browser and select *Create Shortcut* to place a shortcut link on your Desktop.

3.3.7. Change How you View File Lists

You can change how your files are shown in a folder by clicking on *View* then choosing between *Thumbnails, Tiles, Icons, List* or *Details*.

3.3.8. Create Taskbar Chortcuts

Drag a file, folder or shortcut on to the Taskbar for quick access to programs, files or web sites.

3.3.9. Change Desktop Background

Right click on your Desktop and select *Properties*. Click on the *Desktop* tab, pick a new Background and click *Apply* to change your wallpaper.

3.3.10. Take a Screen Snapshot

Press *Print Screen* to take a snapshot of the whole screen or *ALT* and *Print Screen* for just the current window, then paste it into an image editor such as Paint to save it as a picture file.

3.3.11. Make Web Pages Easier to Read

To make text on web pages easier to read, click on *View* (or *Page* in Internet Explorer 7) then *Text Size* and choose a larger size.

3.3.12. Use BCC

To send an e-mail to several people at once without showing all their addresses at the top of the e-mail, use the BCC (Blind Carbon Copy) box in your e-mail client.

3.3.13. Burn CDs/DVDs Safely

When writing a CD or DVD leave your PC alone, as using other programs at the same time could interfere with the burning process.

3.3.14. Alter Music Speed

In Windows Media Player, click the *View* menu then *Enhancements* and *Play Speed Settings*. Move the slider to speed up or slow down a song.

3.3.15. Picture Slideshow

Open a folder of pictures and from the Explorer menu on the left click *Picture Tasks* and then *View as a slideshow*.

3.3.16. Change Volume

Change your speaker volume by clicking on the *Start menu* and *Control Panel,* then click *Sounds and Audio Devices* to change your sound settings.

3.3.17. Open Zip Files

In Windows XP, open compressed Zip files by double-clicking them. Click and drag the files inside out to another folder or the Desktop to extract them.

3.4. COMMON PROBLEMS IN COMPUTERS

A list of common computer problems and solutions. Categories include Virus and Spyware, Browsing the Web, E-mail, Windows and Programs.

3.4.1. Virus and Spyware

How to check if I have a virus or spyware?

There is a free online scanner available to check if you have any virus or spyware on your PC.

What Can I Do to Keep My PC Safe Online?

Keep Windows updated regularly by visiting the Microsoft web site. Use a firewall and anti-virus and spyware removal programs, and use Firefox instead of Internet Explorer.

3.4.2. Browsing the Web

How can I check if a web site is safe to visit?

Internet Explorer 7 and Firefox 2 feature built-in tools to warn you about malicious sites.

What can I do to keep my child safe on the Web?

There are several steps you can take to keep children safe when using the Internet.

Why has my browser homepage changed?

If when you start your browser it loads a different web site instead of your normal homepage, it is possible a malicious program has hijacked your browser and set a different homepage.

To change it back, click on the *Tools* menu then *Internet Options*. On the *General* tab, under the section *Home page* you should see an *Address* box. Type in the address of the site you want (or click Use Current for the site you are currently viewing) and click OK.

3.4.2.1. My Browser Window Opens Too Small

Your web browser remembers the size it was last used at, so if you or a web site have changed the size it will appear like this the next time you start your browser.

To set the correct size, start your browser and hold your mouse over the corner of the window until you see the resize arrows, then click and drag to change the size, then close the browser. When you next start your browser the window should open at the same size.

3.4.2.2. Some Web Sites Do Not Display Correctly

If particular web sites are not displaying correctly - with errors, missing buttons or images, links that do not work, incorrect layouts - this may be due to your browser security settings, which can block parts of a web site it decides are potentially unsafe (though there may be nothing wrong with them, it is just being cautious).

To change security settings in Internet Explorer click on the *Tools* menu then *Internet Options,* but be careful as changing to a low security setting might let unsafe content through to the PC.

There may just be a problem with the web site itself, in which case try again later.

3.4.2.3. Web Page Text Is Too Small

You can increase the size of text on a web page by clicking on the *View* menu *(Page* in Internet Explorer 7) at the top of the browser window, then select *Text Size* and choose a larger size. This should work with most text on web pages though not all.

3.4.2.4. My Browser Address Bar Has Disappeared

Click on *View* from the menu at the top (or *Tools* in Internet Explorer 7) then *Toolbars.* Click to tick the *Address Bar* option and it should reappear.

How can I get rid of pop-up adverts?

To stop adverts opening in new windows you need a pop-up blocker. Both Internet Explorer and Firefox have built-in pop-up blockers. In IE go to *Tools > Pop-up blocker* to turn it on or change your settings.

How can I tell if a web site is secure before buying?

To know whether a site is secure before you give your credit card details, look at the address bar and make sure the web address begins with https://

There should also be a padlock symbol on the address bar (or at the bottom of the page in older versions of Internet Explorer) to indicate the site is secure.

How do I print only certain text or images from a web page Rather than printing out a whole web page, you can select the particular text you want and copy it to a Word document, and then print it out.

Start Microsoft Word and minimize it by clicking on the minimize button at the top-right of the window. Now open your web browser window and click and drag your mouse pointer across the text you want to highlight it. Right-click and *Copy*. Return to Word by maximizing it from the taskbar, right-click and *Paste*. You can repeat this process as many times as you like to get all the text you want into one Word document.

You can copy and paste most images in the same way by right-clicking on the image and clicking *Copy*. Alternatively you can choose *Save As* to save a picture to somewhere on your PC, for example the Desktop or My Documents. Then in Word, click *Insert* then *Picture from File*. Click to select the picture you have saved then click *Insert*.

You can then *Print* your document. By using Word you also have the ability to rearrange, edit and resize text and images before printing.

3.4.2.5. Web Page Won't Print Properly

Sometimes when you try to print a web page it prints incorrectly, for example the right edge of the page may be missing. Look for a Printer-friendly page option, or try printing in Landscape mode in *File > Page Setup*.

You can also try reducing the size of the default right-hand margin in Page Setup. Alternatively copy and paste the areas of the page you want into Word and then print from there.

In Internet Explorer 7 there are improved printing features. Text can be automatically shrunk for printing so all web page content fits on the printed page.

3.4.2.6. Web Page Not Found 404 Error

This common error message indicates that the address or link you have used is incorrect, or it points to a page that no longer exists or has been moved.

Why does online music or video keep cutting out?

Music and audio on the Web often loads some of the content and starts playing while the rest of the file is still being downloaded. This means you don't have to wait too long to hear/see anything, but sometimes you may catch up with it and it has to stop until it has downloaded the rest of the data.

If you find this annoying, you could press pause and then wait for the loading bar to reach full before playing the file. Also if you are using Windows Media Player you can go to *Tools > Options > Performance* and increase the buffer size.

3.4.3. E-mail

3.4.3.1. How Can I Stop Getting Spam?

You cannot completely remove the possibility of receiving spam but there are steps you can take to help reduce the number of unwanted e-mails you receive.

3.4.3.2. I Can't Open My E-Mail Attachments

Outlook Express can block some attachments if it thinks they might be viruses and they will appear greyed out. If you are sure you want to allow these attachments, go to *Tools > Options > Security* and un-tick the box *'Do not allow attachments to be saved or opened that could potentially be a virus.'* Click OK.

If you can access a particular attachment but can't open the file on your PC, you may not have the necessary program installed to run that type of file. You need to ask the person who sent you the attachment what program they used to create it, or ask them to save it in a more common filetype if they can.

Alternatively use a search engine to try to find the necessary program depending on the filetype extension, for example an attachment filename that ends in *.ppt* will require Powerpoint.

3.4.3.3. My Photographs Are Too Big to Send as E-Mail Attachments

Read E-mail Attachments to find out about reducing the file size of images to send as e-mail attachments.

3.4.4. Windows

My PC has stopped responding! What do I do?

If a program or window on your PC seems to have frozen up and you cannot close it by clicking the *X* (Close) button in the top-right corner, hold down the *CTRL* and *ALT* keys together and tap *DELETE* once.

In *Windows Task Manager* click *on Applications* which shows all the programs that are currently running. You can usually tell which program has frozen or crashed as its Status will appear as *Not responding.* Click to highlight that program on the list then click on *End Task.* The PC will now attempt to close it. If it is successful you can then close Task Manager and the PC should be able to carry on as normal.

If Task Manager does not appear, try holding down *CTRL, ALT* and *DELETE* and keeping all three keys held. This will restart your PC, which will often fix the problem. If these keys don't work, you will have to press and hold the power switch or turn the plug off. Turn the PC back on. Your PC should be alright but always try to avoid switching off without shutting down properly first.

I'm running out of disk space. How do I clear out unnecessary files?

Read Clean Out And Clean Up Files to learn about removing unnecessary files. I have deleted a file by mistake! What can I do?

First check the *Recycle Bin* on your Desktop to see if it is in there. Deleted documents go there first, so if you find it there and want to put it back where it was, right-click it and select *Res tore*.

Once items are deleted from the Recycle Bin you will need special software to retrieve them, such as Recover My Files.

I can't find a particular file or folder but I know it's on my PC somewhere!

Click on the *Start menu* and *Search all files and folders*. Type in the name of the missing file or folder and Windows will try to find it.

I can't see any system files or folders! Where are they?

Important system files and folders are usually hidden to prevent accidental deletion. They still exist but will not be visible.

To see them, open any folder and click on *Tools* then *Folder Options*. Click on the *View* tab and under the *Advanced Settings* list tick *Show hidden files and folders*. Also un-tick *Hide protected operating system files*. Now click *OK*.

3.4.5. Programs

How do I get rid of a program I don't need anymore?

To remove a program you need to uninstall it from your PC. Click on the *Start menu* then *Control Panel*. Click on *Add/Remove programs*, select the program from the list and click *Remove*.

Alternatively, go to your *Start menu* and in your programs list, find the entry for the particular program and click on the link to *Uninstall* the program.

3.4.5.1. File Won't Open

Sometimes when you double-click a file, nothing happens or the program that is usually used to open that type of file can't run it. Instead, right-click the file and use *Open With..* to choose a different program to try to open it with. See also Common Filetypes.

3.5. USEFUL PROGRAMS AND UTILITIES

This page is a list of links to web sites where you can download useful programs. There is also a brief description of what each one does.

The various software tools below can be used to remove viruses, create music, play video files, browse the Web, and compress files and more.

- Ad-Aware - spyware remover
- Adobe Reader - read PDF files
- Audacity - sound editor
- AutoReplace - replace text in multiple files
- AVG - anti-virus
- Buzz - music creation program
- Coffee Cup Free FTP - FTP program
- Div X Player - play DivX media files
- D osBox - DOS emulator
- Extract Now - Zip/archive handler
- FileZill a - FTP program
- G IMP - image editing
- HT MLKit - HTML tools

- ICQ - messaging tool
- IrfanView - image browsing/conversion
- KeyNote - notepad and information manager
- Media Player Classic - play music and video files
- Monkey's Audio - lossless audio compressor
- Mozilla Firefox - web browser
- Notepad++ - Notepad replacement
- pen Office - Microsoft Office alternative
- pera - web browser
- RazorLAME - mp3 encoder
- Samurize - desktop enhancements
- Spybot - spyware remover
- Winamp - media player
- WinRAR - RAR archive handler
- WinZip - Zip archive handler
- Zone Alarm - Firewall software

3.5.1. The Best Free Software

This article features information about open source software that you can download free, and can be used as an alternative to expensive commercial programs.

3.5.1.1. What Is Open Source

If you want to write a letter on your PC, play videos, create music files, or edit images, you need to use a piece of software to help you perform that task and that usually means shelling out cash.

However, there is an alternative - a huge range of software available on the Internet to carry out virtually any task you can think of. And it's absolutely free.

Open source software is software whose code is made available to anyone who wants to copy or modify it. This way, the software can adapt, evolve and improve through input from its community of users.

3.5.1.2. Where to Download

SourceForge.net is the first place to look to find and download open source software. Categories include desktop applications, games, multimedia, and security.

Wikipedia features a large list of open source software in categories such as data storage, document editing, education, games, media, networking and security.

3.5.1.3. Ten Useful Programs

10 of the best open source software are listed below:

- OpenOffice.org - office suite, alternative to Microsoft Office
- Mozilla Firefox - web browser, alternative to Internet Explorer
- GIMP - image editing, alternative to Photoshop
- Notepad++ - text editor, alternative to Windows Notepad
- phpBB - build messageboards
- RazorLAME - encode audio to mp3s
- Audacity - audio file editing
- Media Player Classic - play music and video files
- FileZilla - transfer files
- 7-Zip - file compression

3.5.2. Create Documents in Microsoft Word

A beginner's guide to using Microsoft Word to create documents and work with text and graphics.

Why Use Microsoft Word? Microsoft Word is a word processor which can be used to edit many types of document including letters, essays and web pages. You can type text, choose different sizes, fonts, and colours; you can also insert graphics and add tables and charts.

3.5.2.1. Getting Started

Open Microsoft Word by clicking on *Start > All Programs* and selecting Microsoft Word from the list.

Word will open with a blank document. You will see the flashing cursor at the top left corner of the page, ready for you to start typing.

If you hold your mouse over any of the icons in the menu bars or toolbars, you will see a quick description of what those buttons do.

If you can't see any of the toolbars mentioned in this article (mainly the Standard and Formatting toolbars), you may have to instruct Word to show them by clicking *View* then *Toolbars* and putting a tick by any toolbars you want to show.

If you can't see any of the buttons mentioned below on your toolbar, look for the 1 button at the edge of the screen. This is the *More Options* button which will allow you to select which buttons you do or don't want to display.

3.5.2.2. Using Templates

You can save yourself some time by using some basic Templates and Wizards to help you construct your document.

From the *File* menu, click *New* and select the option for *Word Templates*. You can select from a range of document types including letters, brochures and memos, all laid out ready for you to insert your own text. You can also choose to use Wizards that work by asking you questions about the document you wish to write.

3.5.2.3. Working with Text

To select a piece of text you have typed, you need to highlight it by holding the left mouse button and dragging your mouse over the words. Alternatively, if you doubleclick a word, that word is selected, and if you triple-click anywhere on a line, the whole line will be selected. You can change the look and layout of your selected text using the Formatting toolbar at the top of the screen.

3.5.2.4. Inserting Graphics

From the *Insert* menu, select *Picture* then *From File*. You can then browse to the location of an image file on your hard drive. When you have selected the one you want, click *Insert* to place it in your document.

To insert Clip Art into your document click on the *Insert* menu, *Picture* then *Clip Art*. Select the graphic you want from the galleries available and click *Insert* to place it in your document.

To resize an image, click once to select it then click and drag the handles that appear around the edges of the image. If you use the corner handles the proportions of the image will stay the same as you resize it.

3.5.2.5. Printing Your Work

You can preview your work to see how it will look when printed. Choose *File* then *Print Preview* or click the button. To return to the normal view click *Close*.

You can select your printing options (such as which pages to print and how many copies to make) by clicking on *File* then *Print*. To print your work immediately without making any changes to your standard settings, press the button.

3.5.2.6. Saving Your Work

When you want to save your work, choose *File* then *Save As*. You will be asked to give your document a name, and should you need to you can also change the filetype from its default setting (Word Document) to save as a text file or Web page instead.

When saving the same document later, you do not have to use Save As each time, instead you can select *File* then *Save,* or just click on the ™ button.

3.5.2.7. When You Have Finished

Once your work is saved, you can close the document by clicking on *File* then *Close.* You may be asked if you want to save any changes you have made. Click *Yes* if you have made any changes to your document since the last time you saved it. To start another document, click on *File* then *New* or press the button. To open an existing file such as the one you have just saved, click *File* then *Open* or press the button. Locate the file you want and click *Open.*

To exit Word completely, use the X *(Close)* button at the top-right of the window.

There is a lot more to discover in Word and it is a powerful program. Click the *Help* menu for more information and tips. Not only is it easy to use and capable of playing many different types of Audio and Video files, it is also free. Go to www.winamp.com and click the *Download* link then click *Get Basic* (Free). Next choose the *Full* version of Winamp. You may be taken to another web site (such as Download.com), click *Download Now* and save the file to your hard disk.

3.5.2.8. Installing Winamp

Double-click the file you downloaded to begin installation. Click *I Agree* on the license agreement and then choose the *Full* install and click *Next.* Now you can choose which icons you want, and which filetypes should be associated with Winamp so it is the default player for those media types. If unsure, leave them all ticked (except any software or music offers) and click *Next.*

Leave the Destination Folder as it is and click *Next*. If you have several user accounts on your PC, you can set up Winamp to use *Separate settings per user account*. Otherwise choose *Shared settings for all users* and click *Next*. Now you will be asked to select your Internet connection type, for most users this will be the default *Always connected* setting. Click *Next* to proceed.

You can now choose the 'Skin' you want. This determines the theme or look of Winamp. The default *Modern* should be selected unless your PC is a very slow machine, in which case try the *Classic* skin instead. You can always change the Skin later in Winamp by going to *Options > Preferences > Skins*. Click *Install* to begin the installation process. You will be asked to reboot your PC so save any work you have open and click *OK*. Your PC will now restart.

3.5.2.9. Using Winamp

Double-click the shortcut to Winamp on your desktop. Alternatively, use the *Start menu > All Programs* list and look for *Winamp*. The first time Winamp starts you will see a User Information window. Tick *Do not ask me again until next install* and click *Later*. You can now use the *Add Media to Library* option to point Winamp at any folders you have on your computer that contain music or video files. This allows the program to create a library of all your media files for easy access. Otherwise tick *Do not show me this again* and then click *Close*. Winamp has several parts which appear in different windows such as Playlist Editor, Media Library and Video. These windows can be arranged to suit you by clicking on the title bar of the window and dragging it to where you want. Close a window by clicking the X in the top-right corner. If you can't see these windows, click *View* and put a tick by the windows you want to appear.

Winamp supports many types of audio files such as .WAV and .MP3. To start playing some music, click *File* then *Play File* in the main

Winamp window, browse to a song file and double click it. It should automatically start playing.

You can also click and drag a song file to the main window to start playing it now, or alternatively drag several song files to the Playlist Editor window where you can queue up a list of songs to be played one after the other. In the Playlist Editor window you can click and drag songs up and down the queue.

Double-clicking any music file will automatically open Winamp and start playing. Alternatively, select a folder or several song files, right-click and you should see an option to *Enqueue in Winamp*. These tracks will now be added to the playlist.

The main window features song control buttons such as *Skip track forward/back, Play, Pause,* and *Stop.* There is also a volume slider as well as buttons to *Repeat* songs and playlists after they have played, or *Shuffle* the playlist so the songs are played in random order.

3.5.2.10. Video Files

Winamp also supports various Video filetypes such as .MPEG and .AVI. As with audio files, you can double-click, or right-click and select *Play in Winamp* to start playing. The Video window will automatically appear if it is not already open. Right-click the Video window to choose screen size and other video options. Click and drag the corners to resize the window.

3.5.2.11. Playlists

If you wish to save a playlist you have created, click the *Manage Playlist* button and choose *Save Playlist.* You can print a copy of your playlist by clicking the *Misc* button and selecting *Misc* then *Generate HTML playlist.* This opens up a Web browser window with a page containing your playlist, and you can then print it out by going to *File* and *Print* from your browser menu.

If you close Winamp, when you open it later you may find the last playlist you played is still in the Playlist Editor window. Hit *CTRL+N* if you want to clear the current playlist and start a new list.

3.5.3. Write CDs and DVDs

This guide describes how to use DeepBurner Free to burn data or audio to CD or DVD.

3.5.3.1. Introduction
There are many commercial CD/DVD writer programs that you can use which offer a lot of features for creating data and audio CDs and DVDs. This tutorial uses a simple free program called DeepBurner Free. CD/DVD writer drives are able to "burn" discs so that you can create your own data, music or video discs, especially useful for backing up large amounts of data.

There are two main categories of writeable discs you can buy: Recordable discs such as CD-R or DVD-R or DVD+R are discs that can only be written once, whereas Re-Writeable discs such as CD-RW or DVD-RW or DVD+RW can be written over many times.

3.5.3.2. Install DeepBurner
Download the DeepBurner Free program from www.deepburner.com.

Double-click the file you downloaded to run the install program. During setup, use the *Next* button to move through the options screens.

Select your language and agree to the License Agreement. Leave the destination folder as it is, and select the *Full* setup.

Leave the program group as DeepBurner, and wait for the program to install. If you want to, you can read the Read Me file which contains some information about the program. When ready, click *Finish*.

3.5.3.3. Getting Started

Insert the recordable or re-writeable CD or DVD you want to burn into your drive.

The program can be started by double-clicking the DeepBurner desktop shortcut, or by clicking on the *Start menu* then *All Programs > DeepBurner > DeepBurner.*

First you will need to choose whether you want to burn a Data CD/DVD or an Audio CD.

A Data disc can contain any kind of file and is useful for storing and backing up your PC files. An audio CD is like an album you buy from a shop; it stores music files as audio tracks and can be played in a CD player or on your PC.

3.5.3.4. Data Disc

To burn a disc of data files, select Create data CD/DVD and click *Next*.

The New Project window will appear and you will be given the option of creating a multisession disc. If you choose this option, it means you can burn more files to the same disc at another time, if not you will have to start from the beginning and burn all the files again.

Now on your desktop, double-click the My Documents icon or open a new window, and locate the files you want to burn.

Click and drag the files from the window into the DeepBurner box below where it says Name, Size and Description.

You can continue adding the files you want to burn to this list, but keep an eye on the bar below which shows how much space your files will use up on the disc. An average CD allows a total of around 650MB - 700MB and an average DVD is around 4.7GB.

When you are finished, click the Burn disc icon from the menu on the left, then click the Burn button to begin writing your files to the CD/DVD.

To ensure burning is successful, it is best not to run other programs and to leave your PC alone until it has finished.

Time Remaining shows how long before the burning is finished. When it is done, the disc will be ejected.

When the message 'Burn completed successfully. Please insert next disc' appears, click Cancel and then close DeepBurner. Click AW if asked to Save Changes.

3.5.3.5. Audio Disc

If you want to burn a CD-R disc of music tracks, select *Audio CD* as Project Type. Click and drag song files such as MP3s into the box in DeepBurner, as with data files.

With Audio CDs you can rearrange the files into the order you want them to play on the CD. Click to select a particular track and use the arrow buttons above to move the file up or down the list.

When finished, click the *Burn Disk* icon and click the *Burn* button.

DeepBurner will now convert your song files into audio tracks and then start writing them to the CD.

3.5.3.6. Erase Re-Writeable Disc

On the Burn disc window, the *Erase* button allows you to wipe a RW disc so it is blank ready for burning.

Use *Quick erase* unless you have previously stored private data on the disc, in which case it may be better to use *Full erase* to completely remove any trace of the previous data.

3.5.3.6.1. Compress Files

Some files can be too big to be quickly transferred across the Internet or between PCs.

This guide describes how to use the WinZip program to compress files for easier transfer and storage.

3.5.3.7. What Is WinZip?

When transferring files from computer to computer via cable, disk or Internet, it is often necessary to "compress" files to make them smaller so they can be sent more quickly. The files are not damaged or changed, just stored in a different way. A good analogy is to think of it like taking a large letter, folding it up and putting it inside a small envelope. You send the envelope which now takes up less space, but at the other end the envelope can be opened and the large letter folded out again.

This is the advantage of using compressed files. You take a large file or group of files, compress and place in one small compressed file, then send. At the other end the contents can be "extracted" back to their original size and used as normal.

WinZip is the most well-known of many programs able to compress files, in this case to what are known as Zip files which have the filename extension .zip

3.5.3.8. Installing WinZip

You can download a trial version of WinZip from www.winzip.com.

After the trial period is over you will be reminded to purchase a License to continue using the program.

Choose a site to download from and click Download Now. Choose to *Save To Disk* and choose a location on your computer to save to.

Double-click the WinZip file you have downloaded to begin installation. Click *Setup* then *OK* to install to your Program Files folder. As you proceed through the setup options you will need to click *Next* to move on to the next screen.

Click *Yes* to agree to the License Agreement. You can now view or print a Quick Start guide if you wish to. Choose *Start with the WinZip Wizard*.

Choose *Quick Search* and after a few seconds WinZip will finish making a list of your folders. The setup will also need to associate WinZip with various filetypes. When WinZip Setup has finished, click *Close*.

3.5.3.9. Using WinZip

To start the program, double-click the WinZip shortcut on your desktop, or alternatively click on the Start menu then *All Programs > WinZip > WinZip*.

Click on *Use Evaluation Version*. You should now see the WinZip Wizard, which helps you perform the most common tasks associated with WinZip. Click *Next* and for this example, *Create A New Zip File*.

Choose a filename such as "ZipTest" which will be saved to the default folder, or use *Browse* to choose a different folder, enter the filename and click *OK*.

Click *Next*. Use the *Add Files* button to add the files you want to compress, or you can click and drag them into the empty box. When you have added the file or files you want to compress into this Zip file, click *ZipNow* then *Finish*.

WinZip will close and if you now look in My Documents or whichever folder you specified earlier, you should see a *.zip* file called "ZipTest." To open this or any other Zip file, in Windows XP you can double-click it as if it were a normal folder. From here you can drag the files out, which will extract them so they can be used as normal.

Alternatively, right-click the file and choose *Open with WinZip*. Click *Evaluation Version* and you should see the Wizard again.

Click *Next* then *UnZip or Install from "ZipTest.zip."* Click *Next* and choose a folder to extract the contents of the Zip file to (the default location is a folder called Unzipped in My Documents).

Click *Unzip Now*. In the folder you specified you should now be able to see the files you originally compressed in the Zip file, extracted and ready to use again. Click *Finish* in WinZip to close the program.

3.5.3.10. More Help

For more information about WinZip's other features, read the QuickStart guide or click on *Help* from within the program.

3.5.3.10.1. Start Using Internet Explorer 7

Internet Explorer 7 is the latest version of Microsoft's free web browser. This guide explains how to set it up and how to use the new features.

3.5.3.11. Introduction to IE 7

Internet Explorer 7 (IE 7) is the long-awaited new version of Microsoft's leading web browser. It has been designed to be much safer, it has new features to improve browsing and it has better handling of web page code.

IE 7 is free to download and also features optional plug-ins so that you can add tools for improving things like downloading and security.

If you currently use a different browser such as Firefox, you can install IE 7 without affecting your other browser.

Users of Windows XP with Service Pack 2 can download the IE 7 setup file from this link: Download Internet Explorer 7.

If you have Automatic Updates enabled on your PC you will receive IE 7 as an update. You will be given the choice to install the program or not.

Alternatively, visit www.windowsupdate.com and choose the *Express* install option which will download any necessary updates including IE 7.

3.5.3.12. Features of IE 7

IE 7 has a number of improvements over previous versions of the browser:

- Tabbed Browsing: Open multiple sites within the same window and use tabs to move between them
- Pop-up Blocker: Prevents pop-up windows advertisements
- Phishing Filter: Warns you about dangerous fake web sites
- RSS Feeds: Shows RSS news feeds available on a site
- Printing: Automatically fit web page text on the printed page
- Zoom: Magnify parts of a web page to read more easily
- Search Box: Search with your preferred search engine from within the IE 7 window
- Favorites Center: Easy access to your Favorite bookmarks
- Security: Color-coded warnings and security information about the site you're visiting

3.5.3.13. *Installation*

If you downloaded the Internet Explorer setup file, double-click it to begin installation. Click *Run* if you get a security warning.

You should temporarily switch off any anti-virus or anti-spyware security programs you have running. Usually there will be an icon on the taskbar that you can right-click and choose *Close* or *Exit*. Remember to make sure they are switched back on after IE 7 has been installed - often this happens automatically after restarting your PC.

Click *Next* and then *I Accept* on the agreement screen. Now you will be asked to confirm your copy of Windows is genuine by clicking the *Validate* button.

The next screen allows you to install the latest Windows updates. Click *Next* and any necessary updates will be downloaded and installed. This may take a few minutes.

When IE 7 has finished installing you will need to restart your PC. Save any work and click *Restart Now*.

3.5.3.14. Starting IE 7

Start IE 7 using any existing Internet Explorer shortcut you have on the desktop or from your *Start Menu* under *Programs > Internet Explorer*.

If you use ZoneAlarm or other firewall program you may need to confirm you want to allow this changed version of Internet Explorer to access the Internet.

3.5.3.15. Customize Settings

You will now see a page allowing you to customize your settings.

First choose your default search provider (your favourite search engine). This will be used for the Search Box that appears in the top-right of the IE 7 window. Tick to either use your current provider or select from a list of other search providers.

There are several optional settings you may wish to set now:

- Phishing Filter - tick to turn this on. It will warn you about dangerous fake web sites
- See webpages more clearly - the Clear Type option attempts to make text easier to read. If you find it makes it too blurry you can turn it off later
- Help customize webpages to your current location - you can choose your region and language to help web sites show location-specific content
- Help improve Internet Explorer - this collects data as you use IE 7, although it should be anonymous it is recommended you leave this blank

Now click *Save Settings*.

On the next screen you have three choices: take a quick tour to learn about IE 7's new features, choose to install optional plug-ins, or go straight to your homepage.

If you choose the plug-ins option you will be taken to www.ieaddons.com where you can download add-ons that improve browsing, such as tools for filling out forms automatically, media players and download managers.

3.5.3.15.1. Navigating IE 7

The new-look IE 7 includes some big changes to the menus and icons so it's worth spending a little time learning what they are. You can do this by holding your mouse over the menu buttons and reading their descriptions.

The *Forward* and *Back* arrows remain in the top left and there is also a drop-down list of recent pages. Below these are the *Favorites Center* and *Add To Favorites* buttons for managing your site bookmarks.

The *Stop* and *Refresh* page buttons now appear to the right of the Address bar.

A new feature for IE7 is the *RSS* feed icon which shows you any RSS news feeds available on the site you are visiting. If there is a feed available the icon will appear orange. To add a feed to your subscriptions, click the down arrow by the icon to select a feed and then click *Subscribe to this feed*.

You will notice the typical Windows file menus no longer appear in IE 7 (though you can bring them back by pressing the *ALT* key), and there have been other changes too - for example, the old *View* menu is now the *Page* menu.

In the *Page* menu there are options for changing *Text Size* (which you can also do by holding the *CTRL* key, and then either using the + and - keys or your mousewheel) and also an option to *Zoom* which allows you to magnify part of a web page. The Zoom option also appears at the bottom-right of the screen on the Status Bar.

You can access your browser settings by clicking on the *Tools* menu. Click *Windows Update* to get the latest security updates for Windows. Click *Internet Options* to access a range of options including the ability to set your homepage. Click on the *Advanced* tab for more detailed options.

If you have ClearType on and you do find text is too blurry, un-tick *Always use Clear Type for HTML* under the Multimedia section on the *Advanced tab.* Click *OK* to save your settings. You will need to close then restart IE 7 for the change to take effect.

3.5.3.15.2. Tabbed Browsing

Tabbed browsing is a feature new to Internet Explorer but common in other browsers such as Firefox and Opera.

This allows you to open multiple web pages in the same IE window that you can switch between by clicking on their respective tabs at the top of the screen.

To try this, instead of left-clicking a web page link, right-click it and select *Open in New Tab,* or alternatively press your middle mouse button.

A new page will be opened but your current page will still be on-screen. You can access the new page by clicking on the new tab which appears at the top above the page, and has the page's title. To close the tab, click the X button on the tab or right-click and *Close.*

You can keep one tab open and close all others by right-clicking it and selecting *Close Other Tabs.*

To the left of the tabs is an icon called *Quick Tabs* which appears when you have more than one tab open. Click this to see at a glance all the pages you have open.

If you try to close IE 7 when you have multiple tabs open you will be asked if you are sure you want to close all the pages you have open.

3.5.3.16. Managing Favorites

Favorites have also changed in IE 7. Now there is a Favorites Center for organising your site bookmarks.

Click the *Favorites Center* button at the top left of the screen and the Favorites window will appear over the left of the site you are visiting. To fix it in a separate window pane away from the page as in IE 6, click the *Pin the Favorites Center* button in the top right of the Favorites Center window.

You can use the *History* drop-down menu to find sites you have visited before.

To add a site to your Favorites list, right-click the page and select *Add to Favorites,* or click the *Add to Favorites* button at the top left of the screen.

3.5.3.17. Printing

Printing has been improved in IE 7. Now pages will be automatically resized so that all content fits on the printed page.

You can set margins, paper size and orientation by clicking the drop down arrow to the right of the *Print* icon and then selecting *Page Setup.*

You can also remove the header and footer from the printed page.

3.5.3.17.1. Security

There are a number of new security features that have been introduced in IE 7, to make this a much safer browser than IE 6 which had many security flaws and vulnerabilities.

The built-in Pop-up Blocker prevents pop-up advertising windows, and the Phishing Filter lets you know if you are visiting a site that is a security risk and may attempt to trick you into giving your personal information.

The Address bar will change colour to show if a web site might be dangerous -yellow means you should proceed with caution, whereas red indicates a known phishing site and you should not proceed.

The Padlock icon which used to appear on the status bar below a web page now appears next to the address bar. Clicking on the Padlock gives you more information about the site to help you decide if it is safe to use.

You can clear your browsing history at the end of a session by clicking on the *Tools* menu then *Delete Browsing History.*

You can then choose what to delete - your History of visited sites, Passwords, data entered in Forms, Cookies which save your web site preferences, or Temporary Internet Files.

Temporary Internet Files are web site files - such as images and media - that are stored so that the same files do not have to be re-downloaded each time you visit a site.

However, these temporary files can build up over time and end up using unnecessary disk space, so it is worth deleting these occasionally.

Although Internet Explorer 7 is a much safer browser than previous versions, it is still important to protect your PC online and to make sure you install security software and keep it up-to-date.

3.5.3.17.2. Browse the Web with Firefox

The free Firefox web browser offers a safer alternative to Internet Explorer for visiting web sites.

3.5.3.18. What Is Firefox?

Mozilla Firefox is an alternative to the Internet Explorer web browser. The way it has been created means it is safer to use and more flexible than Internet Explorer.

It is free to download and also features optional extensions so that you can add tools to improve things like downloading and security when browsing the Web.

Firefox 2.0 was released in October 2006 and brings new features including Phishing protection and Tab History.

You do not need to remove Internet Explorer to install Firefox - in fact it is useful to have both available to choose from, as there are one or two websites that require Internet Explorer to use, such as Windows Update.

You can have Firefox use the same settings and Bookmarks (Favorites) you had in Internet Explorer.

Firefox's Features:
- *Tabbed Browsing* - instead of opening a separate browser window for each site you want to visit, you can open multiple sites within the same window and use tabs to move between them
- *Add-Ons* - download a range of useful plug-ins to improve browsing and security
- *Download Manager* - organizes your downloads by showing them in a single window
- *Pop-up Window Controls* - allow or suppress pop-up windows
- *Privacy Options* - change settings for handling cookies and clear your history of visited sites
- *Phishing Protection* - warns you if visiting a fake site that may attempt to steal your details
- *Session Restore* - if your system crashes, you can restore your previous session (open windows, tabs, text in forms, in-progress downloads)
- *Tab History* - restore tabs you have accidentally closed
- *Search Box* - search within the browser with your favourite search engine and get suggestions as you type
- *Inline Spell Checking* - check spelling of text you enter in forms

3.5.3.18.1. Installing Firefox

Mozilla Firefox can be downloaded from www.mozilla.com.

Click on *Download Firefox - Free* at the top of the page and save the file to somewhere on your computer (e.g., the Desktop or My Documents).

Close your browser and double-click the downloaded Firefox Setup file to begin installation.

Click *Next* through the various screens and click to accept the License Agreement.

Choose the *Standard* setup type. Wait while Firefox is installed then click *Finish*. Firefox will now launch. If you use ZoneAlarm or other firewall program you may need to confirm you want to allow Firefox to access the Internet.

If you have a version of Firefox already installed, the setup program will check if you require any updates for your browser plug-ins.

3.5.3.18.2. Starting Firefox

Firefox will start automatically after install. To start Firefox in the future, double-click the Firefox shortcut icon on your desktop or go to your *Start Menu* and click on *All Programs > Mozilla Firefox > Mozilla Firefox*.

3.5.3.18.3. Importing Your Internet Explorer Favorites and Settings

Firefox can import your existing settings from Internet Explorer.

From the menu at the top of Firefox, click on *File* then *Import* and choose Microsoft Internet Explorer.

Firefox will attempt to import your Bookmarks (Favorites), cookies, stored passwords, and other data.

3.5.3.18.4. Tabbed Browsing

One of Firefox's most useful features is the ability to open more than one web page at a time within the same browser window and then use 'tabs' to move between them.

This saves you having to have lots of browser windows open at the same time to move between several different web sites or pages.

Try this by right-clicking on any web link (either on a web page or from your Bookmarks list) then select *Open Link In New Tab*. If you have a mouse with a middle-button, pressing this on a link will open a new tab too.

At the top of the browser window, below the address bar and directly above the web page, you should now see tabs with the names of the pages you have open. Left-click on one of the tabs and the main window will change to show the page you have selected. This way you can have many different web pages open at the same time.

To close a tab, click the Close *(X)* button or right-click it and choose *Close Tab*. Click *Close Other Tabs* if you want to close all tabs except this one.

3.5.3.18.5. Restore Closed Tabs

In Firefox 2.0 you can re-open tabs that you have accidentally closed by clicking on *History* then *Recently Closed Tabs*.

Choose the page you want to restore. This will re-open the missing page and put its tab back on the Tab bar.

3.5.3.18.6. Managing Bookmarks

On the top menu click on *Bookmarks* then *Organize Bookmarks*. Here you can organise your favourite site links.

Click *File* in this window and you can create new Bookmarks and folders, and import and export your Bookmark lists.

When finished, close the Bookmarks Manager window. Now if you click *View* then *Sidebar* and select *Bookmarks,* your list of Bookmarks will be displayed along the left-hand side of the browser for easy access.

To bookmark a web page, right-click on the page and choose *Bookmark This Page*.

3.5.3.18.7. Change Options

Click on the *Tools* menu then *Options* and you can change your settings for browsing, security and downloading files. Click on one of the tab headings for specific options:

- Main: here you can set your homepage and the location of your downloaded files
- Tabs: change how tabbed windows are handled

- Content: contains pop-up blocker options
- Feeds: handle RSS news feeds
- Privacy: change your privacy settings and clear your browser history
- Security: change your options for security features and passwords
- Advanced: accessibility, updates and connection options

3.5.3.18.8. Change Text Size

To change the size of web page text to make it easier to read, click on *View* then *Text Size* and increase or decrease the size of the text.

Alternatively, hold the *CTRL* key and scroll your mouse-wheel up or down to adjust the text size.

Depending on the way the particular web page was created, this may not work with all text, especially text you see in logos or other images.

3.5.3.19. More Help

You can use the program's *Help* menu to find out more about Firefox's features, and to *Check for Updates* to the browser.

3.5.3.20. How to Use Search Engines

This article explains how to find what you are looking for online with the help of a Search Engine web site such as Yahoo or Windows Live Search.

3.5.3.20.1. Introduction

If you don't know the exact address of a particular web site, or you have a topic in mind but don't know what web sites exist about that topic, then you need to use a Search Engine.

A Search Engine is like a catalogue of web sites where you can type some words and the Engine will search and then present you with a list of web sites relevant to your search.

3.5.3.20.2. Popular Search Engines

There are many different search engines available, among the most popular are:

- Windows Live Search
- Yahoo
- Ask
- Google
- Altavista
- Hotbot
- Looksmart

3.5.3.20.3. Example Search

This example will show how to use Windows Live Search to search for the web site homepage of popular online auction site eBay.

If you don't know the exact address of the eBay site, this is where a search engine comes in useful. Type in www.live.com into your browser address bar to go to the Windows Live Search web site.

Since you are looking for the eBay web site, type the word *eboy* into the search box. You don't need to type any capital letters when searching.

Press the *Enter* key on your keyboard and Live Search will look for web sites about your subject, then present you with a list of the results.

At the top of the results you will sometimes see Sponsored Links. These are links paid for by companies to ensure their web site is at the top when you search for certain words.

However, these are not always the most appropriate sites to match your search request. The proper results based on your search are the ones just below the sponsored links.

You should notice that the web site at the top of the list is www.ebay.com. If you now click the underlined title link of that result, you should find yourself at the eBay homepage.

If a search result you click is not what you are looking for, click the *Back* button of your browser to go back to the results page and try a different link, or a completely new search.

3.5.3.20.4. What Kinds of Things Can I Search For?

In the search box you can type anything you like - words, names, places, dates; you can even type questions or problems, for example *my mouse has stopped working.*

Try to be as specific as you can if you have a particular problem, for example if you know your mouse is made by the company Logitech, typing *my logitech mouse has stopped w or king will* give you results that are more relevant to your particular problem, and hopefully on one of the web sites you should be able to find a solution.

Search engines will often ignore common words and phrases such as *where* or *what is.* So for example, typing *where is the eiffel tower* will have the same result as if you just typed *eiffel tower.*

3.5.3.20.5. Advanced Searches

In some search engines, near to the search box you will see other options to narrow your search to particular files such as Images.

Click this and when you type a search into the box, the search engine will look for picture files only. Click on Web to go back to searching for web pages.

Some search engines have a link to *Options* or *Preferences* to allow you to be more specific in your searches and select the type of results you want to receive.

The *SafeSearch* filtering option available on certain search engines is especially important as it enables you to filter out or to allow explicit text or images to appear in your results.

3.5.3.21. Using Operators

Most search engines allow you to use what are called *Operators*. These are query words that have special meaning to the search engine, such as AND.

For example, typing in *dog AND cat* forces the search engine to find pages that contain both the words dog and cat. More information about advanced search features can be found on this Live Search help page: Advanced Search Options

3.5.3.21.1. Create and Backup Favorites

This guide explains how to create and backup your Favorites bookmarks.

It also shows how to arrange these links to your favourite web sites into folders.

3.5.3.22. What Are Favorites?

When browsing the World Wide Web you will come across certain web sites which you might want to visit again. Instead of typing in the address each time, you can store a list of *Favorites* in Internet Explorer which require only a simple click to take you to a web site.

3.5.3.23. View Favorites

To view your current list of Favorites, in Internet Explorer 6 click on the *Favorites* menu at the top of your browser. In Internet Explorer 7 you can access your Favorites list by clicking on the *Favorites Center* button.

3.5.3.24. Add a Favorite Site

To add the current web site page to your list of Favorites, right-click somewhere on the page and select *Add to Favorites* from the menu that appears. Alternatively, in Internet Explorer 7 you can also click the *Add to Favorites* button at the top left of the screen.

A new window will open allowing you to give this Favorite a name to help you remember what the site was about. Type it into the *Name* box.

Use the *Create In.*, menu if you want to place this Favorite in a particular category on your Favorites list. If you want to create a new category, click the *New Folder* button and give it a name, for example 'Shopping Web Sites.'

Click *OK (or Add m* Internet Explorer 7) and you should now have a new Favorite link in your Favorites list. Clicking once on this link will take you straight back to this page in future, without having to type the address in again.

3.5.3.25. Creating Folders for Groups of Favorites

As your list of Favorites grows longer, you may find it useful to group together similar links in folders. When you click on the name of a folder in your Favorites list, it will expand to show all the links you have stored in that category.

Click the *Favorites* menu (in Internet Explorer 7 click the *Add to Favorites* button) and select *Organize Favorites.*

Click *Create Folder.* Give it a name then click *Close* and you should see a new folder in your list of Favorites. You can also *Delete* or *Rename* folders in this Organize Favorites window.

To move one of your existing Favorites into a folder, just click and drag the Favorite into the folder.

Folders, like individual Favorites, can be rearranged by clicking and dragging them up or down the list.

3.5.3.26. Backing Up Your Favorites

You can keep a backup of your Favorites in case you accidentally delete any of your list. You can also use this backup to transfer your Favorites list to a different PC or another browser program.

Click on the *File* menu (in Internet Explorer 7 click the *Add To Favorites* button) then click *Import and Export.* You should see a window welcoming you to the Import and Export Wizard. Click *Next,* then select *Export Favorites.* Leave the main folder selected on the Export Favorites Source Folder screen and click *Next.*

Make sure *Export to a File or Address* is selected, then *Browse* to a location on your hard drive where you wish to store a copy of your Favorites list. Type a name for your backup, for example *MyFavorites* and click *Save.* Click *Next,* then *Finish* and a window should tell you the export was successful.

The Favorites backup file is saved as a web page file and it can also be opened in your browser like a normal web page by double-clicking it. It will appear as a simple-looking web page containing your Favorites links.

3.5.3.27. Importing Favorites

To import a Favorites list, go back to the Import and Export Wizard. Choose *Import Favorites,* click *Next,* then make sure *Import from a File or Address* is selected. *Browse* to your saved Favorites file and click *Next.* On the Import Favorites Destination Folder screen, click *Next* then *Finish.*

You should see a message telling you your Favorites have been successfully imported from the backup file.

3.5.3.28. Storing Your Favorites Online

There are a number of web sites which allow you to store your bookmarks online, so you can access your favorite sites wherever you are:

- Windows Live Favorites
- Yahoo! Bookmarks
- MyBookmarks
- Spurl
- Google Bookmarks

3.5.3.29. Back Up E-mails in Outlook Express

This article describes how to back up your Outlook Express e-mail files and how to retrieve them later.

3.5.3.29.1. Introduction

It is important to make a backup copy of your e-mails regularly, as with all your important files. You can keep a copy of your files in another folder on your PC, or back up to a CD for extra peace of mind.

This shows you how to make a copy of the files Outlook Express uses to store your mail data, and then how to import this saved information back into Outlook Express later.

3.5.3.29.2. Find Your Store Folder

First, you need to find the location on your PC where Outlook Express stores your files.

Start Outlook Express and on the menu click *Tools* then *Options*. Click on the *Maintenance* tab then the *Store Folder* button.

This shows you where your messages are stored. Right-click on the location text and choose *Select All*, then right-click on the text again and choose *Copy*.

Click *Cancel*, then *Cancel* again to close the Options windows. Now exit Outlook Express.

Click on your *Start menu* and then click *Run*. Right-click anywhere in the Open box and *Paste* the location you copied into the box. Click *OK*.

3.5.3.29.3. Back Up Your E-Mail Files

In the new window you can see the files Outlook Express uses to store your information.

From the menu at the top click *Edit* then *Select All*. The files in this folder should all now be highlighted. Click *Edit* again and this time choose *Copy*.

Now you need to find somewhere to keep your backups. In this example you will create a new folder in My Documents. For extra safety you may want to store your back up on a CD or another PC.

Open My Documents, click the *File* menu and choose *New* then *Folder*. Give this folder a name, such as 'email backup.'

Double-click this new folder to open it. Now click on the *Edit* menu at the top and then click *Paste*. This will copy your e-mail files from the Outlook Store folder into your new backup folder.

3.5.3.29.4. Restore Your Mail from a Backup

You can retrieve mail you have saved in your backup and import it back into Outlook Express.

Start Outlook Express and from the menu select *File* then *Import* and choose *Messages*. Select the e-mail program that you backed up from (for example, if you used Microsoft Outlook Express 6, choose this from the list). Click *Next*.

Select *Import mail from an OE6 store directory* and click *OK*. Click the *Browse* button and find the backup folder you created (or the CD or other location where you have stored your backup). Click to highlight this folder then click *OK*. Click *Next* to proceed.

You can now select *All folders* (to import all the mail from the backup) or *Selected folders* (to restore only specific mailboxes). Click *Next* then *Finish* to complete the importing of your data.

If you see an error message such as 'No messages can be found in this folder,' make sure the files you are trying to import are not read-only. This can happen if you are trying to restore mail from a CD-ROM.

You can check this by opening the folder or location of your backup files, selecting *Edit* from the menu at the top and then *Select All.* Now click *File* then *Properties.* Make sure the Read Only box is not checked and click *OK.* Now try restoring the backup files again.

3.5.3.29.5. E-mail Attachments

This guide explains how to attach files to messages you want to send by e-mail. There are also tips on what to do with attachments you receive from other people. What are Attachments?

When you send an e-mail it is possible to send other files along with it, such as images or documents. You 'attach' the file by selecting the file on your PC and then use your e-mail program to upload the file into your e-mail account, so it can be sent along with your message.

3.5.3.29.6. Sending Attachments

This example shows how to send a file to a friend along with a message describing it. The instructions are for Hotmail but it should be a similar process with most other e-mail programs or web services.

Log in to your e-mail account and click on *New Message.* Fill out the To: and Subject boxes and write your message. Now click on *Attach* and select *File.*

You now need to tell the computer where to find the file you want to attach. Click on the *Browse* button. When you find the file you want, click to select it then *Open.* Now either click *OK to* confirm, or click *OK and Attach Another* if you want to add more than one file.

Your file will now be uploaded (transferred) to the Hotmail server and should appear listed between the Subject and Message boxes under the list of Attachments. It also tells you how large the file is in MB (megabytes). With a free Hotmail account you can send up to 10 MB in one message, though the larger the file the longer it will take the recipient to download your attachment at their end.

You can now send the message as normal and the attachment file will be sent with it.

3.5.3.29.7. Making Large Files Smaller

Large files will take longer to send and receive. To check how large a file is before you send it, right-click the file on your computer and click *Properties*. Here you can see the file size. If the total of all the files you want to send is over 10 MB you will not be able to send them all at once in Hotmail.

There are several ways to reduce the size of pictures and other files.

3.5.3.29.7.1. Picture Files

Probably the most common type of file attachment is picture files. Normal picture files are called Bitmap files with the filename extension .bmp. These can take up a lot of file space, so to reduce this they are often compressed into smaller-sized filetypes which may loose a little quality, but are usually still good enough for most purposes. Most picture files on the Web or sent by e-mail are .jpeg or .gif files.

To convert an image to one of these compressed filetypes, right-click a picture file and choose to *Open With..* and select Paint. Alternatively right-click the file and choose *Edit* to use your default graphics editing program.

In Paint, click *File* and *Save As.,* and in the *Save As Type* drop-down menu, select a filetype such as JPEG. Give the picture file a name then click *Save* and the picture will be converted to this filetype.

jpeg file sizes can be many times smaller than typical .bmp files. If you right-click the new file you have saved and view *Properties* you should see a difference in file size compared to the original.

With pictures that are very tall and very wide, even .jpeg file sizes can be very large. The solution in this case is to resize the picture down to a reasonable size.

Open your original picture in Paint again and click on *Image* then *Stretch/Skew*. Now you can type in a percentage to stretch the file by. If you input a figure less than 100% you are actually squeezing rather than stretching, for example if you type 50% for horizontal and 50% for vertical then click *OK,* the picture will be squeezed to half of its original size.

This is a simple way of reducing a picture's physical size and therefore file size. Once you have squeezed the picture to the size you want, save it as a .jpeg as before and when you view the file's Properties again the file size should be much smaller.

3.5.3.29.8. Other Files

Other files such as Word documents (.doc files) will need to be compressed into .zip files with a program such as WinZip. Read Compress Files for more information.

However, not everyone will know how to open a .zip file. If they have Windows XP they should be able to open it by double-clicking it. If not, they may have to download a program like WinZip to actually open the file you have sent them.

3.5.3.29.9. Opening Attachments Safely

You should be very careful when opening any file attached to an e-mail. This is one of the most common ways for viruses to travel on the Internet and if you are not careful your PC may become infected. There are some simple rules to follow to keep yourself safe:

- Don't open any e-mail attachments you're not expecting especially if you don't recognise the sender's address
- Don't assume that because it's from a friend's address it will be safe
- Always download the file to your computer first then virus check it before opening it

Hotmail automatically scans all attachments for viruses although it is still possible some infected files will come through. When you click on an e-mail with an attachment, if it is a picture file it may automatically open and appear along with the message.

If you want to save any type of attached file on to your computer, click on the name of the attachment under the Subject heading at the top then click *Download File*.

If it is a picture file it may be opened in a new window, if so right-click the image and select *Save Image As.,* to save to your computer. For other types of files, after you click *Download File,* choose *Save To Disk* to save to your computer.

Once saved, you should scan the file with your virus checker before opening it.

3.5.3.29.10. Printing Image Attachments

If you want to print a picture file you have been sent, download it to your computer then right-click and open with Paint, adjust the height and width if necessary by using *Stretch/Skew* as described above and then click on *File* then *Print.* You can click *Print Preview* to get an idea of how it will look before you print it.

If you have been sent several images (such as a collection of holiday photos) you may want to put them all together to print on one page. One way of doing this is by opening Microsoft Word then clicking *Insert* then *Picture from File.* Do this for every picture you want to include and you should see them laid out on a page.

If you click on a picture in Word to select it, you can then click and drag the corner handles to stretch or squeeze the image, this way you will be able to adjust the pictures until they all fit on one page for printing.

3.5.3.30. *Preventing Spam*

This guide explains what Spam mail is and how to avoid receiving this type of junk mail.

3.5.3.30.1. What Is Spam?

Spam is the term used to describe junk mail messages sent to your e-mail account.

You may receive an e-mail and not recognise the address of the sender. Alternatively, spam mails can come from people you know, but who are not aware their account is being used by a malicious program to automatically send out junk mail to contacts in their address book.

Someone may forward a spam e-mail to you thinking it is a genuine message -perhaps appearing to be from a charity asking for your help to spread their message to everyone you know.

Like junk mail that comes through your door, spam e-mails often try to encourage you to buy a product or sign up for a service. Often there will be an attached file or a link to a web site, but these may actually be trying to install malicious software on your PC or attempting to get your personal information.

3.5.3.30.2. How Can I Tell If a Message Is Spam?

Spam mails will usually try to entice you to open them by having titles that promise things like financial rewards, health products, the latest news or gossip, cheap deals or celebrity pictures. Often their titles will contain odd mis-spellings; these are attempts to fool anti-spam programs.

The safest course of action is not to open any e-mail you're not expecting, especially if it has an attached file, or if you do not recognise the name or address of the sender.

If you have opened an e-mail and are trying to determine if it is genuine, you could try copying the subject line or some of the message into a search engine. If other people have mentioned it on any web sites you should be able to find out if it is spam. You should always do a search on any company before you buy from them or send them any money.

3.5.3.30.3. What Is Phishing?

Phishing is the process of sending out lots of fraudulent spam e-mails with the hope of tricking a few people into giving out their passwords or personal information.

Phishing messages may appear to be from a bank or other financial institution, asking you to confirm your account details by replying to their e-mail or by following a link to a web site.

When you arrive at the fake site, which can often look professional and genuine, you will be asked to type your details into a form and this is where your information will be captured by the criminals behind the phishing.

You may be able to tell if you are not actually on your bank's real web site by looking at the address of the site in your browser.

Remember, your bank will never ask for your passwords or personal information in this way, and if you are in any doubt you should always contact your bank before giving out your details.

3.5.3.30.4. How Did They Get My E-Mail Address?

It may be that the spammer has just made a lucky guess using software which automatically generates possible e-mail addresses.

If your e-mail address is fairly obvious it can be guessed easily. Try to use combinations of numbers and letters, and the longer or more obscure the address the harder it will be to guess.

When you register on a web site or sign up for things like newsletters and membership accounts you may actually be opening the door to receive e-mail marketing spam from these sites and their partners. Most trustworthy sites should give you the option of not receiving advertising mails when you sign up.

3.5.3.30.5. What Can I Do to Prevent Spam?

Because it takes so many different forms, it's virtually impossible to block all spam from appearing in your e-mail account, but there are ways to avoid receiving a lot of it and even help in the fight against the spammers.

Your e-mail provider may have its own system which attempts to filter out a lot of the spam you might otherwise receive. They do this by automatically checking your e-mails for common spam messages, keywords or known spammers' addresses, then place any they find in a separate Spam/Junk/Bulk folder rather than your Inbox.

It is worth having a quick look through your Spam folder occasionally in case some legitimate e-mails have been falsely identified as spam by the system. There is usually an option to move the mail back to your Inbox, or even mark it as *Not Spam* to help the system identify e-mails that are safe to receive.

Some providers allow you to mark any junk mail you do receive in your Inbox as *Spam* to help prevent you getting it again and to stop others receiving it too.

3.5.3.30.5.1. How to Protect Your E-Mail Address

You may want to consider having more than one e-mail address: use one address whenever you sign up for anything on the Web, and give your other address only to people you know.

When you do get spam mail, never reply or click a link offering to remove you from their mailing list. This will only confirm your address is real and you will then get even more spam.

Never sign up for any spam e-mail opt-out lists, these are just another attempt to get your email address or money.

It is important that you have up-to-date anti-virus software. If a virus infects your PC it may try to use your address book to spread itself through e-mail spam to all your contacts.

Visit www.getsafeonline.org for more advice about spam prevention and security online.

3.5.3.30.6. Anti-Spam Software

- BopSpam
- MailWasher
- Spam Bully
- BitDefender Internet Security
- McAfee Internet Security Suite

3.5.3.31. Set Up Instant Messaging

This article describes how to install Windows Live Messenger to send and receive messages instantly.

3.5.3.31.1. Introduction

Instant Messaging allows you to chat in real-time with your friends and other contacts across the Internet.

It is similar to using e-mail, but much easier and you can get a response straight away, provided you are online at the same time as your contact.

Using a program called an Instant Messenger, you can see which of your contacts are currently online and begin a conversation with them.

3.5.3.31.2. Install Windows Live Messenger

Windows Live Messenger is Microsoft's new Instant Messaging software, replacing the popular MSN Messenger.

You can download it free from the Windows Live web site: Download Messenger.

Click the *Get It Free* button. On the window that pops up, *Run* to begin installing as soon as the program has been downloaded. Click *Run* if you get a security warning.

You should now see the Setup Wizard window. Click *Next* and then click to accept the Terms of Use. Click *Next* to move on.

There are now options for several additional features. Leave *Windows Live Messenger Shortcuts* checked if you want shortcuts to the program on your desktop and taskbar. Uncheck the other three options *(Windows Live Sign-in Assistant, MSN Home* and *Windows Live Toolbar)* and click *Next.*

Windows Live Messenger will now be installed. Click *Close* when informed the install has been successful.

3.5.3.31.3. Logging In

A Messenger window should now appear, and you will also see a new icon on your taskbar.

In this new window you will be asked to enter your login information. This is your Windows Live ID (your MSN/Hotmail e-mail address and password).

If you don't have a Windows Live ID, click the link underneath for *Get a new account.* You will then be taken to a web site where you can sign up for a free account (see Set Up A Hotmail E-mail Account for more information).

Once you have entered your login details in the Messenger window, you can tick the options underneath if you are happy for Windows to remember your details and log you in automatically in the future. You should leave these options unchecked if you are using a public PC, or one that other people have access to.

Click *Sign In* to get started.

3.5.3.31.4. Using Messenger

You will now see the main Messenger window on the left, which includes your list of contacts, and a news window on the right.

If you don't want to see the news window every time you start Messenger, check the box under the right window that says *Don't show this window when Windows Live Messenger starts.*

To get started with Messenger, you have to add contacts by entering their e-mail addresses. Click the *Adda Contact* icon at the top, to the right of the *Find a contact or number.,* box.

If you are ever unsure what a particular icon on the screen represents, hold your mouse cursor over it without clicking to get more information.

In the Add a Contact window, you can enter details for the person you wish to communicate with. Type their e-mail address into the Instant Messaging box.

That is all you need to do to add a contact ready to start messaging. However, there are some other options for editing contact details that are worth knowing about.

3.5.3.31.5. Edit Contact Details

Below the Instant Messaging box where you entered the e-mail address, there is an option to *Type a personal invitation.* This allows you to send an e-mail to the person you want to contact with instructions to show them how to install Messenger.

You can enter a nickname for the person which will appear on your list of contacts, rather than their e-mail address, so you can easily see who is on your list. You can also assign them to a specific group such as Friends or Coworkers.

You can add as much information about your contact as you wish by clicking on one of the other menu tabs down the left of the window *(General, Contact, Personal, Work* and *Notes).*

Remember to click the *Save* button when finished adding a contact.

3.5.3.31.6. Send a Message

If your contact is online they will get a message that tells them you have added them to your contact list. The message also asks them if they want to receive messages from you or not.

To start a conversation with one of your contacts, find their name on your contact list. The list shows which of your contacts are currently

Online and which are Offline. If a contact is marked as Online it means they are using the Internet and have their Instant Messaging software running and checking for messages.

If you send a message to someone who is Offline at the time, they will receive your message the next time they access the Internet.

Double-click on the name of one of your contacts to open a conversation window. The box at the top is a record of your conversation so far, and the box below is where you can type your messages.

Click in this box and begin typing like you would an e-mail message, though usually an instant message is shorter than an e-mail so conversations can be quick. You can use the menu icons just above the box to add emoticons, change font size, colour and more.

When finished, click the *Send* button or press the *Enter* key on your keyboard. Now wait for a response. If your contact is online they will get a pop-up message that tells them you want to start a conversation.

Under the message box on your conversation window you will see a notification if your contact is currently writing a reply to you. Their message will then appear in the top box, after the message you just sent. You can continue the conversation by writing your next reply in the message box, and clicking *Send* again.

When you want to finish a conversation, send a message to let your contact know and then click on *Close* in the top-right of the conversation window.

3.5.3.32. Get the Most from the Web

An introduction to the many and varied ways you can take advantage of the World Wide Web - including shopping, education, family history, entertainment and careers.

3.5.3.32.1. Introduction

Shopping, banking, hobbies, dating, health, entertainment, education, careers, clubs, sports, holidays... virtually every aspect of our daily lives can benefit from the Internet in some way. Whatever you need to do, there is usually a way to use the World Wide Web to help you find the information you need.

3.5.3.32.2. What You Can Do Online

You can order your clothes, food and medicine online and have them delivered to your door. Need a plumber? Hairdresser? Use the Web to find local businesses and get directions to shops in your area.

Choose to manage your bank accounts through your web browser, make payments and pay bills. Buy CDs, DVDs, books and clothes without travelling to the shops, and read reviews and other customers' opinions before you buy.

You could book your holiday online, take a virtual tour of a resort before you get there and compare prices to find the best deals. You can get road maps, travel guides and exchange rate information.

Get weather reports and read the latest news and sports results. Find advice and information about health issues and get first aid tips. Write an e-mail message to a friend, or send a photo you've just taken with your digital camera to a relative in another country.

Need to help the kids with their homework? All the information they need is on the Web, with pictures, sounds and games to get them interested.

3.5.3.32.3. Get Entertained

You can read electronic books, poetry and short stories online. Browse works of art or take a tour of a museum. And you no longer need a television to watch TV and films, or a stereo to listen to music or radio. You can do it all on your PC using the Web.

How about a game? You can find thousands of free games on the Internet, and you can play with other people too - from simple puzzle and card games to complex 3D worlds where you can take part in adventures with thousands of other players across the globe.

3.5.3.32.4. Get Educated

There are many ways to improve your knowledge using the Internet and open up new possibilities.

You could learn a different skill or a new language and get a qualification. Look for a new job and display your CV to potential employers. Work from home or start your own business, using the Web to promote yourself and to sell to customers across the world.

3.5.3.32.5. Get Social

Read information about your local area and get involved in your community. Find relatives you never knew you had and discover facts about your past by researching your family tree.

Find out about clubs and societies you could join. Arrange meetings and discuss topics in messageboards with people who share your interests. Make new friends in chatrooms or maybe meet someone special on an online dating site.

3.5.3.32.6. Get Creative

You can find tools to create your own music, games and movies. Design a web site to share your hobby or teach people using your knowledge. Write about your life or become a citizen reporter and use your blog to give the latest news from your area.

The Internet offers fantastic opportunities for everyone, but especially the elderly and those who are unable to leave their homes due to disability or other reasons. For some people it gives them a whole new lease of life.

Pick a search engine such as Google or Yahoo and type some words or a phrase into the search box. You may be surprised how many people share your interests and how much the Web has to offer.

3.5.3.33. Things to Do on the Web

On this page are examples of the types of things you can do on the World Wide Web, with some web sites for you to try.

There are web site links for shopping, news, travel, music, sports, games and more:

- Buy and sell products online - Amazon, eBay
- Learn computer skills - BBC Webwise
- E-mail friends and relatives around the world - Hotmail, Yahoo! Mail
- Research your family history - Ancestry.com, Family Search
- Book holidays - Virgin Holidays
- Find cooking recipes - Delia Smith, Cooking.com
- Read the latest news - BBC News, CNN
- Get information about Sports teams and matches - BBC Sport, Sports Illustrated
- Book theatre tickets - Last Minute
- Find out cinema showtimes - Movie Watcher
- Listen to music from famous bands and unsigned artists - Download.com Music, iTunes
- Get information about health issues - BBC Health, NHS Direct
- Learn a language - BBC Languages, World Wide Learn
- Read about historic events - The History Channel, History World
- Get weather reports - Weather.com, BBC Weather
- Find businesses in your area - Google Local
- View maps of areas and get directions - Yahoo! Maps
- Play games with people around the world - GameSpy, MiniClip
- Listen to radio stations - Web-Radio, BBC Radio
- Watch TV programmes online - wwiTV, Beeline TV
- Watch movie trailers - Apple Trailers, Movie Insider
- Get gardening tips - BBC Gardening, About Gardening
- Get help with homework - BBC Schools, Homework High

- Meet new people and chat with interest groups - FaceParty, Match
- Write about your life, thoughts, hobbies and experiences - Blogger
- Go on virtual tours of museums and art galleries - Louvre, Oxford Virtual Tour

There are many other things you can do on the Web. You can use search engines such as Google or Yahoo to find web sites on whatever topics you are interested in. Have fun!

3.6. USEFUL WEB SITES FOR COMPUTERS

A list of links to web sites where you can find useful information and downloads.

Categories include shopping, sports, e-mail, music and games.

Blogging

- www.blogger.com - write a blog
- www.spaces.live.com - create your space

Computers

- www.dell.com - Dell computers
- www.download.com - download software
- www.tweakguides.com - improve performance

E-Mail

- www.hotmail.com - Hotmail
- http://mail.yahoo.com - Yahoo! Mail

Games

- www.fileplanet.com - game files
- http://pcgameview.blogspot.com - PC games news
- www.gameFAQs.com - game help

Graphics Cards and Drivers

- www.nvidia.com - Nvidia graphics cards
- www.ati.com - ATI graphics cards

Jobs

- www.monster.com - search for jobs

Kids

- www.bbc.co.uk/schools - learning
- www.channel4.com/learning - homework help
- www.kidscom.com - fun activities

Media Players

- www.winamp.com - music and video player
- www.quicktime.com - Quicktime video player
- www.sourceforge.net - Media Player Classic

Movies

- www.imdb.com - movie database
- www.themovieinsider.com - movie news and previews
- www.apple.com/trailers - movie trailers

Music

- www.allmusic.com - music guide
- www.myspace.com - listen to bands
- www.mp3.com - download MP3s
- www.itunes.com - iTunes

News

- www.cnn.com - CNN
- www.bbc.co.uk/news - BBC

Photography

- www.flickr.com - photo sharing
- www.istockphoto.com - stock images

Reference

- www.about.com - general info and articles
- www.wikipedia.org - web encyclopedia

Search Engines

- www.live.com - Live Search
- www.yahoo.com - Yahoo
- www.google.com - Google

Shopping

- www.amazon.com - buy books, music and more
- www.which.net - Which guides
- www.ebay.com - buy and sell items
- www.play.com - buy DVDs

Sound Cards and Drivers

- www.creative.com - Creative sound cards

Sport

- www.sky.com/sports - Sky Sports
- http://news.bbc.co.uk/sport - BBC Sport
- http://sportsilustrated.cnn.com - Sports Illustrated

Web Browsers

- www.mozilla.org - Firefox
- www.opera.com - Opera

Web Design

- www.w3schools.com - tutorials
- www.sitepoint.com - articles and forums
- www.alistapart.com - design tips

Web Hosting

- www.oneandone.com - web hosting

Windows

- www.windowsupdate.com - update Windows

3.7. MAKING WEB SITES - 30 USEFUL TOOLS

3.7.1. Creating Web Pages

- Dreamweaver - the popular web site creation package (Buy)
- Hotscripts.com - free scripts to use in your site (Free)
- HTML Kit - tools for coding web pages (Free)
- AutoReplace - easily replace text across multiple web pages (Free)

- Namo web editor - tools for creating web sites (Buy)
- Notepad ++ - improved version of Notepad (Free)
- Serif WebPlus - web page creation software (Buy)

3.7.2. Designing Graphics

- Photoshop - popular image editing software (Buy)
- CoolText.com - online logo graphics generator (Free)
- IrfanView - image editing software (Free)
- Pixie - show values for any colour on screen (Free)
- Serif Draw Plus - graphics editing software (Buy)

3.7.3. Managing Your Site

- Contribute - easily update sites and blogs (Buy)
- Bro wser Resolution Checker - test your site at different resolutions (Free)
- CoffeeCupFreeFTP - manage and upload your site files (Free)
- Ema il check - check if spammers can see your site email addresses (Free)
- Firefox Web Developer extensions - tools for development of sites (Free)
- FileZill a - manage and upload your site files (Free)
- Link popularit y - see how popular your site is with search engines (Free)
- Lynx browser - check how your site appears in a text browser (Free)
- W3C Validator - validate your page coding against Web standards (Free)

3.7.4. Flash Animation

- Flash Professional - premier Flash authoring software (Buy)
- SWiSH Max - Flash creation tool (Buy)
- A 4 Desk - easily create Flash sites using templates (Buy)
- DVIO - captures video from digital camera to AVI (Free)
- KoolMoves - easily create Flash animation (Buy)
- Turbine Encoder - convert video to streaming Flash (Free)

3.7.5. Other Features

- M SN SiteSearch - add a search facility to your site (Free)
- PHPBB - PHP-based system for creating forums (Free)
- X SPF Music Player - play mp3s on your web site (Free)

3.7.6. 5 Steps to Keep Your PC Safe Online

There are some simple steps you can take to ensure your PC remains protected while you surf the Web.

Following these tips can help protect your PC from virus, spyware and other online threats.

3.7.6.1. Update Windows

Microsoft regularly releases free downloads to fix security problems with Windows, Internet Explorer and other Microsoft software such as Office. Read Update Windows to find out how you can get these important updates.

3.7.6.2. Install a Firewall

A good firewall such as ZoneAlarm will prevent programs from accessing the Internet without your permission, and block access to your PC from intruders. Read Install ZoneAlarm Firewall to find out how to install and set up a firewall.

3.7.6.3. Check for Viruses

Malicious virus code can infect your PC's system files and damage your important data. Read Check for Viruses which explains how to use an anti-virus program to find and remove malicious programs.

3.7.6.4. Remove Spyware

Spyware is malicious code that tracks your movements on the Internet and can even affect your PC's performance. Read Remove Spyware which explains how to get rid of malicious spyware and adware.

3.7.6.5. Browse More Safely

The latest web browsers such as Internet Explorer 7 and Firefox 2 offer security features like pop-up blockers and phishing filters to keep you safe when visiting web sites. Read *Start Using Internet Explorer 7* or *Browse The Web with Firefox* to learn how to install and use these browsers.

CONCLUSION

In this chapter you have studied about the purchase process of computers, installation process purchasing process of computer, insight to computer components, quick tips about computers, common problems encountered in computers and useful web sites for computers.

Chapter 4

HOW TO ASSEMBLE A DESKTOP PC

4.1. TOOLS AND EQUIPMENT

4.1.1. Basic Tools

Before you begin building or refitting a computer, you should have some basic tools:

1. #2 Phillips-head (cross-shaped) screwdriver
2. Needle-nose pliers
3. A large level working space
4. Brush

4.1.1.1. Optional, But Useful Tools

Some other tools and equipment can come in handy as well, such as:

1. Anti-static Wrist Strap *(Highly Recommended)*
2. Spring action parts grabber.
3. Electrical tape
4. Wire or nylon ties

5. Flashlight, preferably hands-free
6. A second, working computer to swap parts, look for tips, ask for help on-line, download drivers and patches, etc. - very useful
7. A can of compressed air - useful when working with older parts that have collected dust. A better alternative but also more costly, is a vacuum cleaner designed for cleaning electronics.
8. Magnetic screwdriver
9. Zip ties or velcro ties for cable management

4.2. PREPARATION

Proper preparation is the key to a successful build. Before you begin, make sure you have all the tools you will need, secure a clear, well-lit workspace, gather all the components you'll be using and unpack them one at a time, verifying that everything that is supposed to be there is actually present. At this point you should leave the parts themselves in their protective anti-static bags, and assemble all the accompanying manuals. Now I know you want to get started, but trust me, *read the manuals*, check the diagrams, make sure you understand where each part goes and how it attaches. If there is anything you don't understand, now is the time to do a little extra Internet research or call the manufacturer with your questions.

Find a dry, well-ventilated place to do your work. You should have plenty of light and if possible, you should choose an area without carpet on the floor, as carpet tends to generate a lot of static. An unfurnished basement is a good work location.

Safety precautions are important for your own security. Please read the safety precautions thoroughly.

4.2.1. Safety Precautions

1. Static electricity is the biggest danger to the expensive parts you are about to assemble. Even a tiny shock which is much too small for you to feel can damage or ruin the delicate electronic traces many times smaller than a human hair that make up your CPU, RAM and other chips. It's important to use your anti-static wrist strap to prevent damage to these components. Once you have the power supply installed in the case, clip the end of the wrist strap to the outside of the power supply. (Never plug your computer in while you are connected to it by a wrist strap.) This will ensure that you, the case and the power supply are all connected to a common ground, in other words there will be no inequality of charge that will allow a spark to jump from you to the case. It's also helpful to have an anti-static mat to set the case and other components on.
2. Nobody but you is at fault if you shock your components with static electricity. Make sure that you take the precautions in the previous paragraph to ground yourself from static electricity. (Note: if you really must work on a computer and have not got proper anti-static equipment, it is *usually* OK if you make sure that you do not move about much; are not wearing any static-prone clothing; handle components by the edges; and regularly (once a minute or so), touch a grounded object.). The *case metal* of your PC's power supply will usually be a suitable grounded object (please note that the metal must be unpainted). As noted above, touch it every few minutes while you are working on your PC if you haven't got a wrist strap.
3. Turn off your computer and switch off your Power Supply at the wall before installing or removing any components - if power is flowing to components as they are installed or removed, they can be seriously damaged. In order to have a

computer properly grounded, you need it plugged in at the wall but turned off at the power supply and at the wall. The neutral line may be earthed.
4. Never cut the grounding pin off your power cord. This "safety ground" stands between you and potentially lethal voltages inside the power supply.
5. Be wary of sharp edges! Many lower-end PC cases have sharp, unfinished edges. This is especially so on interior surfaces, and where the case has been cut or punched-out. Use care and take your time to avoid cutting your hands. If your case has this problem, a little time with some sandpaper before you begin construction can spare you a lot of pain. Be extra careful not to cut yourself when installing the I/O Shield.
6. Dismantling discrete electronic components such as your Power Supply or Monitor is dangerous. They contain high voltage capacitors, which can cause a severe electric shock if you touch them. These hold a charge even when the unit is not plugged in and are capable of delivering a fatal shock.

4.2.2. Construction

Start by putting your case down on your work surface, with the case door facing up, and open the case.

4.2.3. Motherboard

Find the *motherboard standoffs* (spacers) that should have come with the case. They are screws, usually brass, with large hexagonal heads that are tapped so you can fasten screws into the top. These hold the motherboard up off the case preventing a short-circuit. Set these aside.

Remove the I/O Shield from the back of the case where the ports on the back of the motherboard will fit, and put in the I/O Shield that came with your motherboard. There may be small metal tabs on the inside of this face plate, if so you may have to adjust them to accommodate the ports on the back of the motherboard.

Some case styles make it difficult to install the motherboard or the CPU with the power supply installed. If the power supply is in your way, take it out and set it aside (we'll put it back in later).

Now locate the screw holes on your motherboard and find the corresponding holes on the motherboard plate (or tray) in the case. Put a standoff in each of these holes on the tray and position the motherboard so that you can see the holes in the top of the standoffs through the screw holes in the motherboard.

Now is the time to make sure the ports on the motherboard are mating with the backplate you just installed, and make any necessary adjustments. The small metal tabs are intended to make contact with the metal parts of the connections on the back of the motherboard and ground them, but you may have to bend these tabs a bit to get the ports all properly mounted, this is where those needle-nose pliers may come in handy.

If you have trouble lining up the screw holes, double check that you have the standoffs in the proper holes on the tray. With lower quality cases there are sometimes alignment problems and you may have to forgo one or two screws. If this is the case, make sure you remove the corresponding standoffs. Some combinations of motherboards and cases may also use different types of screws in different places or provide non-matching screw holes that cannot be used in a specific case. The motherboard can possibly be damaged if you try to push it into position with the wrong set of standoffs underneath or when trying to use the wrong set of screw holes.

Now fasten a screw through each of the motherboard screw holes into the standoffs underneath. These screws should be snug but not tight, there is no reason to torque down on them, hand tight is fine, otherwise you can damage the motherboard.

Once the motherboard is installed, it is time to plug the other components.

4.2.4. CPU

An example of a CPU socket, LGA1150. This is the previous generation socket for consumer Haswell desktop CPUs and some Xeons.

LGA2011 socket. These processors are used by i7 Extreme and most Xeons. Note that LGA 2011 CPU's are not comparable with its successor (LGA 2011-3) even though they look similar and have the same number of pins.

Installing the CPU, and the CPU's heat-sink and fan, are by far the most difficult steps you'll have to complete during your build. Here, more than anywhere else, it will pay to read the instructions carefully, look at the parts, study the diagrams that came with your CPU and/or third party cooling solution, and make sure you thoroughly understand what you are going to do *before you try to do it*. During the process, if anything does not seem to fit or make sense, put the parts down and look things over carefully before you proceed. Some operations, especially installing the heat-sink/fan combination, can require pretty firm pressure, so don't be afraid to push a little harder if you're sure everything is set up correctly.

The details of the installation process differ in slight but important ways for each manufacturer's processors, and even within a manufacturer's product line. Therefore, for these details, you should rely on the instructions that are provided with the CPU.

The two things that go wrong the most often and most expensively (minimum of a killed CPU, sometimes more) in building one's own computer are both related to the CPU and its cooler:

1. Switching the computer on "just to see if it works" before adding any CPU cooling unit. Without cooling, CPUs heat up at extreme rates (a CPU heats up anywhere between ten times and a thousand times as fast as a cooking area on your stove!). By the time you see the first display on the screen, your CPU will already be severely overheating and might be damaged beyond repair.
2. Mounting the CPU cooler improperly. Read the instructions that came with your CPU and cooler very carefully and ensure you are using all components in the correct order and correct place.

If you buy a third party cooling solution for your CPU make sure you get one that is compatible with the CPU you have. "Compatibility" here just means, "Can you fit it in next to your RAM or whatever else is sticking up in the neighborhood." Most brands come with multiple mounting brackets that will suit many different chipsets, but it is best to check for compatibility just in case.

After the CPU is installed in the socket and secured in place, it's time to add thermal paste and then install the cooler. The plain metal back of the CPU, which is what you're now seeing, is exactly matched by the bottom plate of the cooler. You add thermal paste *only* on the CPU, *never* on the cooler's surface. Very little is needed. The two flat metallic surfaces will spread the paste between them, and it will spread a bit more when it becomes hot. (The cooler surface may have a protective piece of film over it; don't forget to remove it. But see below for the possibility of "thermal pad" being supplied, instead of paste. This is rare nowadays, but *read the instructions*).

A pea-sized dot is the amount usually advised, though some people make a thin "X" on the CPU surface, and some draw a line. (There are numerous videos on Youtube advocating one or another, some with photos using glass plates.) Don't overdo -- you don't want paste squeezing out the edges. Some people suggest spreading paste over the whole surface, then cleaning it off with a razor blade, then adding the pea. The idea is to close invisible imperfections in the metal. This is probably overkill, and involves extra handling of the CPU, never a good idea. Try not to touch the mating surfaces of the CPU and cooler -- the oils from your skin will impede heat transfer.

You should receive a tube or applicator of thermal paste in the CPU or cooler package, some CPU coolers come pre-applied with thermal paste (such as AMD's wraith cooler), you can optionally add your own to the CPU as extra or continue with the pre-applied compound. If your CPU didn't come with thermal paste and the cooler didn't have any pre-applied, thermal paste is readily available from most computer retailers.

If using a thermal pad supplied with your cooler, make sure you remove any protective tape from the die just before installing and do not get it dirty - and do not combine thermal pads with thermal paste, it is either one or the other. Then, check that you install the cooler in the right orientation and that you set it flat on the CPU die without exerting undue pressure on any edges or corners - the latter can make small pieces of the die break off, killing the CPU.

One option you may consider, before installing the heat-sink, is to "lap" the heat-sink, which means to smooth out the bottom surface. To do this, you will need a very flat surface; a piece of thick window glass will work. Fasten your sandpaper on the flat surface, invert the heat-sink on the sandpaper and sand in small circles, applying minimum pressure. Check frequently and when you see a uniform pattern of scratches, switch to finer grained sandpaper (the numbers go up as the sandpaper is finer, so something such as 220 is coarse while 2000 will be very fine).

Remember that you are not trying to remove any material, just polish out surface irregularities. If you get it right, you should have a surface which feels completely smooth to the touch (but don't touch it, the oil in your fingers can cause corrosion of the fresh surface) with a mirror finish. Some companies producing heat-sinks lap the surface themselves, so if the surface already looks like a perfect mirror, leave it alone. A lapped heat-sink is more effective as it will have better surface contact with the chip.

Tighten the cooler using only the specified holding devices - if you did everything right, they will fit. If they do not fit, check your setup - most likely something is wrong. After mounting the cooler, connect any power cables for the fan that is attached to the cooler.

As an aside to the instructions above, it has been my personal experience that fitting the CPU and heat sink is best done on a supportive surface (a telephone directory on a table in my case) prior to installation, to avoid excessive flexing of the motherboard.

A last note: if something goes wrong and the cooler has to be removed (like maybe you realize you didn't take the protective film off the cooler surface), the paste will have to be removed from the CPU for the restart. *Don't panic!* All it takes is a coffee filter (not paper towels or anything else that will leave fibers) and a little isopropyl alcohol (from the drugstore). Thermal paste removes easily with a little gentle rubbing. Work from the outside edge in.

If you've got the CPU and its cooler installed, and the motherboard in the case, you're over the hump, there are just a few more easy pieces to go before that momentous first power-up.

4.2.4.1. Memory Slots

Next, you will need to install your RAM (random access memory). Find the RAM slots on your motherboard; they will look something like the picture on your left. To install the RAM modules, first push on the levers (white plastic in the picture) on either side of the DIMM socket, so that they move to the sides. Do not force them, they should move fairly easily.

Put the RAM module in the socket. Line up the notch in the center of the module with the small bump in the center of the RAM socket, making sure to insert it the right way. Push down on the module until both levers move up into the notches on the sides of the module. There should be a small "snap" when the module is fully seated. Although this does require a fair bit of force, do not overdo it or you may break the RAM module.

4.3. DIFFERENT TYPES OF RAM MODULES

Take a good look at your seated RAM, if one side seems to be higher than the other, odds are it is improperly seated - take it out and try again. As you handle the RAM, try not to touch the copper stripes you can see along the bottom edge, as doing so is the best way to damage the part.

Start adding RAM at the slot labeled "Bank 0" or "DIMM 1." If you do not have a stick in "Bank 0" or "DIMM 1" the system will think there is no RAM and will not boot.

On motherboards with 4 slots, you'll see alternating colours. For example, slot 1 is blue, slot 2 is black, slot 3 is blue, slot 4 is black.

If you were to put 4 gigabyte of RAM in your personal computer, it is best to use dual channel 2 GBx2 sticks. Put the first 2 GB stick in slot 1, and put the 2nd stick in slot 3 (the two slots that are blue) - leaving slot 2 empty. This will give you better performance, than putting 4 GB in slot 1 alone.

4.3.1. Power Supply

Installing your power supply is pretty straightforward, if it came with your case it was pre-installed and if you took it out earlier to get the motherboard in, now is the time to put it back. Otherwise a few moments of screwdriver work will get the job done. Generally there will be a bracket on the top of the case where the power supply is mounted and a few screws used to fix it in place. Some cases place the Power Supply differently, see the documentation that came with yours.

Some power supplies come with modular cables, so you can plug in only those you'll be using; now is a good time to figure out what you'll need and plug them in. Other power supplies have all the cables hardwired in, you'll want to separate out the ones you'll need and neatly coil the remainder somewhere out of the way.

If your power supply has a switch to select 115 V or 220 V make sure it is set properly, this is important. Many newer power supplies can automatically select and don't have such a switch. Once you get the power supply installed make sure you check the motherboard documentation carefully for the location of the power sockets. You may then connect the main power, a 20 or 24 pin plug, into the motherboard. There may also be an additional four or eight pin power lead that needs to be plugged in to the motherboard (the CPU power connector) usually located near the processor socket.

4.3.2. Graphics Card

Insert the card into a matching slot on the motherboard.

If your motherboard or CPU has a built-in graphics adapter you want to use (like Intel HD Graphics), skip this section.

If you have a PCI Express video card, install it into the PCI Express socket. Your computer will have a few of them, but choose the one which is most convenient for you and will allow you to fit it into the desktop case easily. Check your motherboard manual for instructions.

When your card is properly installed the line formed by the top of the card will be exactly perpendicular to the motherboard, if one side seems to be higher than the other, chances are that it is not fully inserted, press a little harder on the high side or pull it out and try again.

4.3.3. Installing Drives

Next install the hard drive and optical drives.
How a drive is physically installed will depend on the case.

- A Serial ATA connector
- Floppy Disk Drive Cable

Most drives are SATA (Serial ATA) which use simple, small cables for a data connection. The ends of the cables are L shaped, just look carefully at the cable ends and the connector on the drive and match them up. Only one drive can be connected to each SATA port on the motherboard. Some SATA drives have two different power ports - make sure you connect ONLY ONE of these ports to the power supply, connecting both can damage the drive.

Older drives have PATA (Parallel ATA) connections which use a flat ribbon (IDE) cable for data connection. When using an IDE cable, plug the two connectors that are closer together into the 2 drives, and the third to the controller or motherboard. The connector furthest from the board should be attached to the drive set as Master. Make sure the drive that you will install your OS on is the primary master. This is the master drive on the Primary IDE bus which is usually the IDE 40 pin port on the motherboard labeled "Primary" or "IDE 1."

Next, plug a 4 pin molex power connector into each hard drive and optical drive. If you are installing the power connector to a SATA drive, some drives have the option of using either the SATA power connector (a flat about 1" wide connector) or the standard molex connector; use one or the other, *not both*. Connecting both can break your hard drive. For better data transfer, you can purchase heat-protected high-end data cables at your nearest electronics store.

Newer SSD's will often use the PCI Express standard; for those, follow the same instructions as you would do for a PCI Express graphics card.

If you install a floppy disk drive, the cable is very similar to the IDE cable, but with fewer wires, and a strange little twist in the middle. Floppy drives do not have master/slave configurations. The floppy disk connector is not usually keyed, making it all too easy to plug it in the wrong way! One wire in the IDE cable will be colored differently: this is pin 1. There is usually some indication on the floppy drive as to which side this is.

The power plug for a floppy is 4 pins in a line, but rather smaller than the standard hard drive power connector. Plug the end of the cable with the twist into the floppy drive ("drive A:"). Plug the other end of the floppy ribbon cable into the motherboard. If you install a second floppy drives, plug the middle connector into "drive B:." The twist between drive A: (on the end) and drive B (in the middle) helps the computer distinguish between them.

4.3.4. Other Connections

Some cables are attached to pins on a board (e.g., motherboard or extension card).

In order to turn the computer on, you will need to connect the power button and while you are at it, you might as well do the reset buttons and front panel lights as well.

There will be a set of pins, usually near the front edge of the motherboard to which you will attach the cables sometimes already connected to the front of the case, or if needed to be supplied with the motherboard. Most of the time the plugs will be labeled as the pins they will connect to in the motherboard, there they can be difficult to read since the print is very small or you may not be in the right orientation to do so. The documentation that came with your case and motherboard should tell where these connectors are.

In addition, you can connect any case-specific ports if they are supported by the motherboard. Many cases have front mounted USB, Firewire and/or sound ports.

Other connections of this type to remember can be power for the CPU fans, various temperature sensors and <u>Wake-on-LAN</u> cables (if the feature is supported) from the network card to the motherboard.

4.3.5. Prepare for Power Up

Some people will put power to a system several times during assembly and for experienced builders this may serve some purpose. For first timers though, it's best to assemble a minimal complete system before powering up. Minimal because that way there are comparatively few potential sources of trouble, complete so that you can test everything at once and because the fewer times you have to put power to an open machine, the better.

If you've been working along with us you should now have such a minimal system put together. Briefly this includes a case with a motherboard in it, a processor (and its cooling unit) and some RAM plugged into the motherboard, hard and floppy drives installed, and some kind of video available. If your motherboard has built-in video, you might want to use that for this first try, even if you are going to install a video card later.

4.4. COMPARISON OF VGA, DVI AND HDMI

Monitors will either have a VGA, DVI, HDMI (see picture, as they are a lot less apparent than PS/2 / USB by comparison) or for newer ones, a Thunderbolt 3/USB 3.1 plug. Most monitors use HDMI connectors, and so most graphics cards have HDMI output. If you have one type of plug and the graphics card has another, you can easily buy an adapter. Some cards even come with one.

There are two standard connectors for mice and keyboards; PS/2 connectors and the more modern USB connectors. Plug the mouse and keyboard in the appropriate slot.

Note: If you intend to install an operating system from a boot CD or floppy, or modify BIOS settings you will need to use either a PS/2 keyboard, a USB to PS/2 converter, or a motherboard that supports USB devices. Otherwise your keyboard will not work until the operating system has loaded USB drivers.

Once you have this all set up, it's time to double check, then triple check that you have made all the necessary connections and that you haven't left any foreign objects (where's that screwdriver?) in the case.

4.4.1. Power Up

Take a moment to check one more time that everything is as it should be. Make sure you've removed your wrist strap, turn on the monitor, then press the power button, and observe the inside of the open machine. (*Do not touch any part of the inside of the machine while it is powered up: you will NOT die but your computer might.*) The first thing to look for is that the CPU cooler fan spins up, if it does not, cut the power immediately. This fan should start up right away; something is wrong if it doesn't and your CPU is in danger of overheating so stop now and troubleshoot.

NOTE: If you have a Gigabyte brand motherboard, the CPU fan may twitch and stop turning. Wait 10-15 seconds and it should start. If it does not, there is a problem and you should immediately cut power as stated above. Other fans such as case fans should turn on and spin.

If the CPU fan spins up, check that all the other fans that should be spinning: case fans and fans on the power supply and video card (if installed) are also spinning. Some of these fans may not spin up until a temperature threshold is passed, check your documentation if anything is not spinning.

If the fans spin, you can turn your attention to the monitor, what you are hoping to see is the motherboard's splash-screen, usually featuring the manufacturer's logo. If you see this, take a moment to bask in the glow, you've built a computer!

If this happy event does not occur, if smoke appears, or if the computer does not do anything, unplug the power cord immediately and check the steps above to make sure you have not missed anything. Give special attention to the cables and power connections. If the computer does appear to come on, but, you hear beeps, listen carefully to the beeps, turn the computer off, and refer to your motherboard's manual for the meaning of the beeps.

Some boards have an optional diagnostic device, usually a collection of LEDs, which when properly plugged in will inform you of the nature of the problem. Instructions for installing this as well as the meaning of its display should be in the manual for the motherboard. If the computer turns on but the only thing that comes on is your power supply, turn it off. This probably means something is shorted, and leaving it on could damage the parts.

4.4.2. Additional Hardware and Peripherals

Now that you have a working system it's time to think about installing an operating system, which is covered in the next section. It's best to leave the installation of additional components (like sound-cards, modems, and second video cards) and peripherals (printers, joysticks, etc.) until after the OS install in order to allow the plug n' play features of the OS to do their trick.

4.4.3. Step-by-Step Guide to Installing Windows 10

4.4.3.1. Installing Windows 10

With Windows 10 for PCs and tablets due end of this month, and the fact that Microsoft is pushing out preview builds left, right, and center recently, we thought it's time to revisit the installation process to see how it differs from previous versions of Windows and the early Windows 10 builds. Of course, this is more for the curious and those who've hung on to previous versions of Windows (ahem, XP); Windows 8.x users and seasoned system builders should have no problems understanding the installation steps.

Before the avalanche of images, here's a quick recap. Windows 10 can be upgraded over Windows 7 and 8.1. For qualified systems, this upgrade is free. We already know that clean installs can be done after the upgrade; and rumor has it that Microsoft would also be offering the OS on a DVD and USB flash drive. For this article, we used the latest preview build ISO, and installed the OS on a empty drive; if you're doing an upgrade, you may or may not see some of these screens.

So, let's begin.

Step 1: This is the first screen you will see if you install Windows 10 using a bootable USB flash drive or DVD. Here's where you choose the OS' language, time and currency format, and input method.

Step 2: It's pretty obvious what you need to click here. Like Windows 8.x, you can also choose to repair your computer.

If you choose the repair option, you will end up at a Troubleshoot screen where you can choose to reset your PC and re-install windows (you can either keep or remove your files), or access more advanced troubleshooting options. For the latter, there are options for doing a system restore (if you've a restore point on your PC), image recovery, running commands in command prompt, and letting Windows fix any startup problems. You can also get to the advanced startup options after installation via the new Settings app in Windows 10.

Step 3: Traditionally, your Windows product key can be found on your online order info, in the confirmation email for your purchase, or on the DVD packaging. That said, this is more for a clean install. If your device has been successfully upgraded to Windows 10, and you choose to wipe your device and do a clean install later, the device will reactivate without the need of a Windows 8.x product key.

Step 4: Accept the license terms. After you read them, of course.

Step 5: Next, you'll be presented with this screen, where you can choose to do either an upgrade (files, settings, and apps are moved to Windows) or a custom install (files, settings, and apps aren't moved). The latter is the one to choose if you prefer a clean install, which was what we did.

(Note: If you're doing an upgrade, and you're running Windows Media Center, Windows 10 will remove it).

Step 6: Here's where you select the drive to install Windows 10 on. You can format a drive here as well.

Step 7: Now, you wait.

Step 8: Before you can start using Windows, there are some personalization, location, browser and protection, and connectivity and error reporting settings that you can adjust. You can zip through all these by using the Express settings, which basically turn everything on, or you can hit the small print that says 'Customize settings' to customize them. We went for the latter.

Step 9: If you choose to customize the settings, the first page deals with your contact, calendar, input, and location data. Read these carefully to decide if you want to turn the settings on or off.

Step 10: The next page deals with browser data, connectivity, and error reporting. Again, read these carefully and toggle the switches accordingly.

Step 11: Next, you need to specify who the owner of the device is. You can choose to sign in with your company ID, which will give you access to your company's resources.

Step 12: Microsoft really wants you to sign in to Windows 10 with your Microsoft account. If you use Microsoft services like Office, Outlook.com, OneDrive, Skype, or Xbox, it makes sense to sign in with your Microsoft account as it ties them all up and makes your Windows experience more personal.

If you use two-factor authentication, you'll need to enter your code. If you don't have a Microsoft account, you can create one right away. Alternatively, you can sign in with a local account. Unlike Windows 8.x, apps like Mail will not force you to switch to a Microsoft account and stop you from using the app if you don't comply.

Step 13: Instead of signing in using your Microsoft account password, you've the option to create and use a short PIN instead.

In addition to easy typing, another benefit is that once created, this PIN only works on the device it's created on.

Step 14: Windows 10 will save new documents and pictures to OneDrive. If you're okay with that, just hit Next to continue. Else, you can click the small text that says 'Save new files only to this PC by default.'

Step 15: You can also decide if you want to turn on the Cortana personal assistant feature. Some people may not want to use Cortana as this allows Microsoft to collect and use their location; contacts; voice input; info from email and messages; browser history; search history; calendar details; and more. If you were to ask us, Cortana is one of the best features in Windows 10. And for it to be truly useful, it has to be granted access to such data. Here's a link to Microsoft's privacy statement.

Step 16: There's no step 16. Welcome to Windows 10!

CONCLUSION

In this chapter you have studied about the explanation of various terms used for computers.

GLOSSARY

Term	Description
Adware	Advertising program often installed along with other programs
Attachment	A file attached to an e-mail message for sending between computers
Blog	Web log. Personal web page where the author can post their views and experiences and receive comments.
BMP	Bitmap. The most common graphics file type for Windows PCs
Bookmarks	List of your favourite web sites
Browser	Software that displays web pages such as Internet Explorer and Firefox
Compression	A method of reducing the storage space a file takes up. Files must be decompressed to be used again
Crash	Occurs when a program causes your computer to stop responding
Demo	Free demonstration version of software that allows you to try before you buy
Directory	An index of web site links arranged in categories

Term	Description
Disk Space	The size of the area on the hard disk where files can be stored
Domain name	URL or Address of a web site on the Internet
Download	Transfer a file from another computer to your own
Driver	Software required for Windows to use a piece of hardware such as a graphics card
E-mail	Electronic mail passed between computers
Favorites	List of your favourite web sites
Firewall	Program or device that blocks or allows Internet access to a network or a PC
Flash	Software to create and play web site animations
Font	Text of a particular size and style
Freeware	Software that is free to download and use for as long as you like
Hardware	Physical parts of a computer system such as the hard disk, keyboard and printer
HTML	HyperText Markup Language. The code that makes up a web page
Home Page	The main page of a web site, often a welcome page
Hyperlink	A text or graphic you click on to go to another page or a different web site
Internet	A collection of inter-connected computer networks
Install	To load and copy program files onto a computer
JPG/JPEG	Compressed graphics file for sending across the Internet
Link	A text or graphic you click on to go to another page or a different web site
Malware	Malicious software such as virus or spyware programs
Modem	Device that links a computer to the Internet through a telephone line

Glossary

Term	Description
MP3	Compressed audio file to save disk space and for transfer across the Internet
Online	Connected to the Internet
Phishing	Fraudulent e-mails trying to trick you into giving out personal details
Plug-in	Extra programs that can be installed into larger programs to handle special tasks, such as playing certain types of movie files in a browser
Podcast	Internet audio broadcast that can be played back on PCs or MP3 players such as the iPod
Pop-Up	Small window that appears on a web page, often used for advertisements
Program	A set of instructions to make a computer carry out a task
Rootkit	Software that hides system files and can allow attackers to access your computer undetected
Router	Device used in home Internet networks to send data from the web to specific computers
RSS	Really Simple Syndication - a system to feed you news stories from web sites
Search Engine	Tool that searches the Web for keywords and provides relevant links
Server	A computer that holds Internet data such as web site files and can send it to another computer when requested
Shareware	Software that is free to download but you pay a fee if you want to continue using it after the trial period
Shortcut	A link you can click to go straight to a particular program or web page
Software	A program or a set of instructions to make a computer carry out a task

Term	Description
Spam	Junk mail messages to e-mail addresses
Spyware	Software that tracks your movements on the Web for advertising purposes without your knowledge
Stream	Start playing music or video as soon as it begins downloading
Surfing	Moving from one web page to another
Trial	Software that allows you to try before you buy
Trojan	Malicious virus program disguised as useful software
Uninstall	Remove program files from a computer
Upload	Send a file from your computer to an online destination
URL	Uniform Resource Locator. The address of a web site on the World Wide Web
Virus	Destructive program that infects and damages computer files
VoIP	Voice over Internet Protocol - voice conversations across the Internet
WAV	The standard audio file type for Windows PCs
Web Page	Individual page on a web site
Web Site	A collection of connected web pages located at a particular domain name
Wiki	Web site that can be edited by users to add information
Windows	Microsoft operating system installed on most PCs
World Wide Web (WWW)	Information space on the Internet stored on servers across the world containing documents connected together through hyperlinks
Worm	Malicious code that uses an infected PC to spread itself to others
Zip	Compressed file format to reduce disk space needed by a file and to transfer it between computers more quickly

COMMON FILETYPES

Below is a list of common file types with a brief description and examples of programs that can open these files.

If a file does not appear to have a filetype extension, open the folder it is stored in and click on *Tools* from the menu, then *Folder Options*. Click on the *View* tab and un-tick *Hide extensions for known file types*.

.avi	video file. Open with *Windows Media Player*
.bmp	image file. Open with *Paint*
.cfg	configuration file.
.dat	data file.
.doc	document file. Open with *Word*
.exe	program file. Double click to run
.gif	image file. Open with *Paint*
.htm	web document. Open with *Internet Explorer*
.html	web document. Open with *Internet Explorer*
.ini	text configuration file. Open with *Notepad*
jpeg/jpg	image file. Open with *Paint*
.mov	movie file. Open with *Quicktime*
.mpeg/mpg	video file. Open with *QuickTime*
.mp3	audio file. Open with *Windows Media Player*
.pdf	secure document file. Open with *Adobe Reader*

.pps	slideshow presentation. Open with *PowerPoint*
.ppt	presentation file. Open with *PowerPoint*
.sys	system file.
.txt	text file. Open with *Notepad*
.wav	audio file. Open with *Windows Media Player*
.xls	spreadsheet file. Open with *Excel*
.zip	compressed file. Open with *WinZip*

KEYBOARD SHORTCUTS

This section features a list of key combinations that can be used to perform special functions.

- *Windows key* - access Start menu
- *Windows key + Pause* - open System Properties
- *Windows key + D* - minimise/restore windows
- *Windows key + F* - open Search window
- *Windows key + F1* - open Help and Support Center
- *Windows key + E* - open Windows Explorer window
- *Windows key + M* - minimise all windows
- *Windows key + TAB* - move through open windows on Taskbar
- *Windows key + SHIFT + M* - restore all windows
- *Hold CTRL while dragging* - make a copy of selected item
- *Hold CTRL + SHIFT while dragging* - make a shortcut to selected item
- *CTRL + ESC* - open Start menu
- *CTRL + C:* Copy
- *CTRL+X-* Cut
- *CTRL+ V-* Paste
- *CTRL + A* - Select All

- *CTRL + Z* - Undo
- *CTRL + B* - Bold highlighted text
- *CTRL + U* - Underline highlighted text
- *CTRL + I* - Italicise highlighted text
- *CTRL + Plus key* - increase browser text size
- *CTRL + Minus key* - decrease browser text size
- *CTRL + ALT + DELETE* - open Task Manager
- *ALT + underlined letters in menus* - open menu item
- *ALT + ENTER* - show Properties of selected object
- *ALT + F4* - close current window or program
- *CTRL + F4* - close window within program
- *ALT + TAB* - switch between open windows or programs
- *TAB* - move forwards through control items or links in current window
- *SHIFT + TAB* - move backwards through control items or links
- *ENTER* - click selected control item or link
- *BACKSPACE* - move up one folder level
- *HOME* - go to start of current line or web page
- *END* - go to end of current line or web page
- *CTRL + END* - go to end of current document
- *PAGE UP* - move up through current document or web page
- *PAGE DOWN* - move down through current document or web page
- *PRINT SCREEN* - take snapshot image of current screen
- *ALT + PRINT SCREEN* - take snapshot image of current window
- *F2* - rename selected item
- *F5* - refresh current window or web page
- *F6* - move through window panes

ABOUT THE AUTHOR

Dr. S. Anandamurugan, PhD
Associate Professor
Department of Information Technology
Kongu Engineering College, Perundurai
Tamilnadu, India
E-mail: valasuanand@yahoo.com

Dr. S. Anandamurugan obtained his Bachelor's degree in Electrical and Electronics Engineering from "Maharaja Engineering College,

Avinashi" under Bharathiyar University and Masters Degree in Computer Science and Engineering from "Arulmigu Kalasalingam College of Engineering, Krishnan Koil" under Madurai Kamaraj University. He completed his PhD in Wireless Sensor Networks under Anna University, Chennai. He has 17 years of teaching experience. He is currently working as an Assistant Professor (Selection Grade) in the Information Technology department of Kongu Engineering College. He got 10 awards. Received "Dr. A. P. J. Abdul Kalam award for Teaching Excellence" award for the year 2017 - 2018 from Marina Labs, Chennai. Received "Best Outstanding faculty" award for the year 2016 - 2017 from Top Engineers, Chennai. Received "Teaching Excellence" award for the year 2016 - 2017 from Indus Foundation, Chennai. Received "Senior Educator and Researcher" award for the year 2016 - 2017 from National Foundation for Entrepreneurship Development, Coimbatore. Received "Outstanding Faculty" award for the year 2016 - 2017 from Venus International Foundation, Chennai. Received "UWA Effluent Star of the Decade" award for the year 2016 - 2017 from CHAPTERed Writers Association, Chennai. Received "Best Paper" award for the year 2016 from International Journal for Modern Trends in Science and Technology (ISSN: 2455-3778) for the paper entitled on "An Energy-Efficient Min-Max Optimization with RSA Security in Wireless Sensor Networks." Received "Best Author" award for the year 2012 - 2013 from Shivam Book Publishers, Chennai. Received "Best Staff" award for the year 2007 - 2008 at Kongu Engineering College, Perundurai. Received "Appreciation award" for producing excellent result in Anna University examinations held in Nov/Dec 2003 by Kongu Engineering College (Citation plus reward). Project entitled on "Automated Irrigation System using Wireless Sensor Networks" selected as a best project by Kongu Engineering College in 2015-2016. Industrial Training attended: 3. Seminar/Workshop Conducted: 10. Conference Organized: 5. Value Added Course conducted: 5. Sponsored Projects carried out: 1, Consultancy Activities: 6. He has written 75 books under various titles and publications. Three of his books are prescribed as Text/Reference books by many leading Universities and autonomous Colleges in India. The book titled on "Wireless Sensor Networks" published by University Science Press, New Delhi is referred in the syllabus of JNTUK and its affiliated colleges, GMR Institute of Technology, Kakinada. The book titled on "Wireless Sensor Networks" published by Satya Prakashan Publisher, New Delhi is referred in the syllabus of University of Mysore. The book titled on "Placement Interviews: Skills For Success," McGraw Hill, New Delhi is referred in the syllabus of JNTUH and its affiliated colleges, All Branches of KIIT University, Bhubaneswar, Odisha, Dr. M. G. R. Educational and Research Institute University, Chennai, Madanapalle Institute of Technology & Science, Madanapalle, AP (Autonomous), Mari Laxman Reddy Group of Institutions, Teungana, Charustar University of Science and Technology, Gujarat, Bharathiyar University, Coimbatore and Paavai Engineering College, Namakkal, Tamilnadu.

INDEX

A

advantages of computers, 6
advertisements, 90, 151
adware, 128
animations, 150
anti-spyware, 90
application software, 45, 46
applications of computers, 7
arithmetic and logic unit, 30
attachment, 74, 107, 108, 110
authentication, 147

B

bandwidth, 44
banking, 9, 117
banks, 9, 18
bar code reader, 13, 20
blogger, 121
blogs, 9, 126
browser, 66, 67, 70, 71, 83, 89, 92, 94, 95, 96, 97, 98, 99, 100, 101, 102, 104, 112, 126, 147, 148, 151, 156
browsing, 77, 89, 92, 93, 94, 95, 96, 98, 102
burn, 59, 84, 85, 86
businesses, 118, 120
buttons, 14, 15, 57, 61, 71, 79, 83, 86, 92, 141

C

cables, 39, 40, 41, 137, 139, 140, 141, 142, 144
cache memory, 32, 33, 36
CAD, 15
CAM, 8
CD-ROM, 34, 106
Central Processing Unit (CPU), 11, 12, 14, 16, 30, 31, 32, 34, 35, 39, 40, 48, 51, 52, 53, 54, 131, 133, 134, 135, 136, 137, 139, 142, 143, 144
characteristics of computers, 3
classification of computers, 5
compiler, 11, 49, 50, 54
computer, v, vii, viii, 1, 2, 3, 4, 5, 6, 7, 8, 9, 11, 12, 13, 15, 16, 17, 20, 21, 23, 30, 32, 33, 34, 35, 37, 39, 40, 41, 42, 43, 44, 45, 46, 47, 48, 49, 50, 51, 52, 53, 54, 55, 56, 57, 58, 60, 62, 63, 64, 65, 66, 67, 69, 82,

87, 96, 107, 108, 109, 110, 120, 128, 129, 130, 131, 135, 136, 138, 139, 141, 143, 144, 146, 149, 150, 151, 152, 157
control unit, 30, 31, 53

D

data transfer, 141
database, 123
digital cameras, 40
Digital Video Interface (DVI), 44, 143
DVI port, 44
Dynamic RAM (DRAM), 36, 37

E

eBay, 100, 101, 120
Electronic Delay Storage Automatic Calculator (EDSAC), 2
Electronic Discrete Variable Automatic Computer (EDVAC), 2
Electronic Numerical Integrator And Computer (ENIAC), 2
e-mail, 9, 56, 63, 68, 73, 74, 105, 106, 107, 108, 109, 110, 111, 112, 113, 114, 115, 116, 117, 118, 121, 149, 151, 152
equipment, 43, 54, 60, 129, 131
ethernet port, 44
evolution of computers, 2

F

firewire port, 43

G

game port, 44
Google, 105, 119, 120, 121, 124
graphic plotter, 21
graphic tablet, 12, 18

H

history, vii, 1, 10, 94, 96, 99, 148

I

impact printers, 24, 28
input unit, 11, 12, 51, 54
interface, 45, 47

J

joy stick, 12

K

keyboard, v, 12, 13, 14, 15, 40, 42, 57, 60, 61, 100, 117, 143, 150, 155

L

laptop, 16, 23, 56, 58
learning, 7, 92, 122
light pen, 12, 16
limitation of computers, 6

M

Magnetic Ink Card Reader (MICR), 13, 18, 19
memory, 11, 12, 19, 21, 31, 32, 33, 34, 35, 36, 37, 38, 39, 40, 48, 51, 54, 58, 59, 137
microphone, 12, 18, 42, 44
Microsoft, 46, 64, 70, 72, 77, 78, 79, 89, 97, 106, 110, 114, 127, 145, 147, 148, 152
Microsoft Word, 46, 64, 72, 78, 79, 110
modem port, 43
monitors, 21, 23, 47, 57, 143

Index

mouse, 12, 14, 15, 16, 17, 40, 42, 57, 60, 61, 62, 71, 72, 79, 80, 92, 93, 97, 99, 101, 116, 143
music, 8, 18, 58, 59, 61, 63, 73, 76, 77, 78, 81, 82, 83, 84, 85, 86, 118, 119, 120, 121, 123, 124, 152
music CDs, 59

N

networking, 78
non-impact printers, 24, 28

O

operating system, 11, 32, 45, 47, 48, 49, 54, 63, 75, 143, 145, 152
Optical Character Reader (OCR), 13, 19
Optical Mark Reader (OMR), 13, 20
output devices, 21, 31

P

parallel port, 42
pop-up windows, 90, 96
port, 11, 40, 41, 42, 43, 44, 140
power connector, 43, 139, 140, 141
primary memory/main memory, 32
printer, 21, 23, 24, 25, 27, 28, 30, 40, 42, 72, 150
programming, 37, 38, 49
PS/2 port, 42

Q

query, 102

R

registers, 30, 31, 33

S

safety, 106, 130, 132
scanner, 12, 17, 20, 42, 49, 70
secondary memory, 32, 34, 35
security, 56, 66, 71, 78, 89, 90, 92, 94, 95, 96, 98, 99, 113, 114, 127, 128, 130
semiconductor, 32, 33, 34
serial port, 42, 43
social network, 7, 9
sockets, 44, 139
software, vii, 9, 11, 44, 45, 46, 47, 49, 54, 56, 75, 76, 77, 78, 81, 95, 111, 112, 113, 114, 117, 121, 126, 127, 149, 150, 151, 152
spam, 73, 111, 112, 113
spyware, 70, 76, 77, 127, 128, 150
Static RAM (SRAM), 36, 37
storage, 32, 35, 36, 40, 41, 47, 51, 52, 53, 58, 78, 86, 149
system software, 45, 47

T

track ball, 12, 16, 17

U

Universal Automatic Computer (UNIVAC), 3
Universal Serial Bus (USB) Port, 40, 42, 43, 58

V

VGA port, 43
video games, 23
videos, 8, 77, 136
viruses, 73, 76, 109
VoIP, 152

W

web, 55, 60, 66, 67, 68, 70, 71, 72, 73, 76, 77, 78, 79, 81, 89, 90, 91, 92, 93, 94, 95, 97, 98, 99, 100, 101, 102, 103, 104, 107, 111, 112, 114, 115, 118, 119, 120, 121, 124, 125, 126, 127, 128, 149, 150, 151, 152, 153, 156

web browser, 70, 72, 77, 78, 89, 95, 118, 128

web pages, 68, 71, 79, 93, 98, 101, 125, 149, 152

web service, 107

web sites, 55, 67, 71, 76, 90, 91, 95, 97, 99, 100, 101, 102, 104, 111, 119, 121, 126, 128, 149, 150, 151

webpages, 91

websites, 95

windows, 63, 71, 82, 94, 96, 97, 98, 105, 146, 155, 156

working memory, 31, 34

World Wide Web (WWW), 102, 117, 118, 119, 152

Independent Component Analysis (ICA): Algorithms, Applications and Ambiguities

Editors: Addisson Salazar and Luis Vergara

Series: Computer Science, Technology and Applications

Book Description: Modern treatment of data requires powerful tools that allow the possible valuable contents of that data to be thoroughly understood and exploited. From the plethora of techniques proposed to achieve those objectives, the independent component analysis (ICA) has emerged as a flexible and efficient approach to model and characterize arbitrary data densities.

Hardcover ISBN: 978-1-53613-994-5
Retail Price: $230

Computational Mechanics (CM): Applications and Developments

Editor: Jacob Yuen

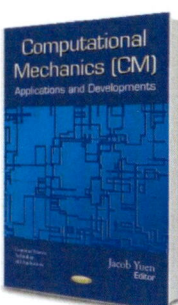

Series: Computer Science, Technology and Applications

Book Description: In this collection, the authors examine how modeling impact of solid particles contributes to an understanding of the fundamental mechanisms of erosive wear. However, most previous studies focus on spherical particles, which are not representative of abrasive particles.

Softcover ISBN: 978-1-53613-672-2
Retail Price: $95

BRAIN-MACHINE INTERFACES: USES AND DEVELOPMENTS

EDITORS: Carla Bryan, Ivan Rios

SERIES: Computer Science, Technology and Applications

BOOK DESCRIPTION: *Brain-Machine Interfaces: Uses and Developments* reports on advances in the development of a speech prosthetic, building on previous data as well as the results of detecting phonemes, words and phrases during overt and covert speech.

SOFTCOVER ISBN: 978-1-53613-368-4
RETAIL PRICE: $82

IoT: PLATFORMS, CONNECTIVITY, APPLICATIONS AND SERVICES

AUTHOR: Abdulrahman Yarali

SERIES: Computer Science, Technology and Applications

BOOK DESCRIPTION: Telecommunications is currently one of the fastest changing industries with broadband networks and service providers aggressively competing in their mature subscription points for churn and value-added services to provide consumer experience for a sustainable return on their extensive investments.

HARDCOVER ISBN: 978-1-53613-400-1
RETAIL PRICE: $230